KARSH & FISHER *see* CANADA

CANADA

as seen by the camera of

YOUSUF KARSH

and described in words by

JOHN FISHER

1960

THOMAS ALLEN LIMITED / TORONTO

CONTENTS

1701

KARSH & FISHER *see* CANADA

NEWFOUNDLAND

1 : NEWFOUNDLAND

NEWFOUNDLAND on the globe looks as if the earth's rotation had cast her adrift from North America to set her sights on Europe. The tenth largest island never moved far from North America, but she is still the closest piece of this continent to Europe. Navigators tell us that the other green isle, Ireland, is just across the pond. In the colour of the soil, the fracture of the coast line and the speech of the natives, Newfoundland is Ireland's North American cousin. But, never, never make comparisons with Newfound-landers, because they are proud of what they are, and if the visitor will understand this fierce pride, the welcome will outdo that found in most other lands.

Newfoundlanders need understanding because they have lived alone in North America longer than any other European people above the Rio Grande. John Cabot raved about the waters teeming with fish five years after Columbus sailed into the Caribbean. Had the Pilgrims sailed north instead of towards New England, they would have found settlers and gardens and fish outfitters in Newfoundland. Indeed, for almost a century before French or English colonies were established on this continent, the Old World markets bid for Newfoundland cod.

For so long Newfoundland was neither European nor North American, but just the great friendly green-topped stepping stone between the two. The trading world came to her harbours because she had the products and the position as she still has. Gander airport in the bush is short-order host to the inter-continental commuters, and no bush airport on earth welcomes such a parade of "big names" as Gander. Movie stars, industrialists, inter-national fixers, United Nations delegates, tourists and traders stop at the crossroads of the airlines. In pre-colonial times the New Found Land was visited by sail as she now is by airfoil.

Newfoundland offers a lesson in both geography and psychology. We think it is far away "out there" because we really don't know enough about

2

. . . the fracture of the coast line

3

the tenth province. If you would like to play a game, put a measuring string on a globe and you'll find that St. John's, Newfoundland, is closer by more than 500 miles to Rio de Janeiro, Brazil, than New Orleans, Louisiana, is. St. John's is closer than New York is to any point in South Africa. When the clock in Ottawa's Peace Tower strikes "twelve noon", it is 1.30 p.m. in St. John's. Yes, even the time zone is unusual—Newfoundland claims only half the time zone named after her, which is one half-hour ahead of Atlantic time.

St. John's, Newfoundland, is roughly on the same latitude as Victoria, British Columbia. It is a few degrees colder in St. John's, but the harbour of this, the oldest French or English settlement in North America, never freezes. The mean temperature is similar to Toronto's, so skaters in St. John's can never depend on the weather to provide firm, natural ice. When they can skate they do so on a pond in the heart of the city, with a delightful ring to its name—Quidi Vidi.

The jaw which Newfoundland thrusts to the Atlantic is hard and rocky, but the names she has applied to her coves and capes are as soft as down. Charming ones—Heart's Delight, Heart's Desire, Heart's Content, Cupids, Angel's Cove, Happy Adventure. Cheerful ones, too—Honey Pot Harbour, Bay of Hope, Too Good Arm, Big Paradise, Little Paradise. Sonorous and pleasing place names—Rose a Rue, Blue Pinion, Avalon, Jacques Fountain. Then there are the names which ring of hardship and misfortune —Bad Bay, Gripe Point, Famish Cove, Slave Harbour, Empty Basket, Bleak Island, Devil's Punch, Bloody Bay, Missing Point, Breakhead Point, Damnable Bay and Muddy Shag.

Newfoundlanders did not bring the old-world names with them. They named their headlands for a feeling of the moment, for some event or to describe. Fox Trap Cove surely comes from fishermen who have passed the word along that the currents in that particular stretch of water are as tricky as a fox and if not watched will trap a boat. Come-by-Chance is a familiar name in Newfoundland and probably means that in sailing Trinity Bay, the sailors came across this particular place by chance. What humour and anecdote lie behind such names as Naked Man, Double Mare, Lion's Den, Whales Gulch, Cavies Nose and Maggoty Cove?

Never will I forget my first visit to a Newfoundland outport, as all little places are named. The houses of this little village far from the noise of the

4

St. John's . . . closer by 500 miles to Rio de Janeiro than New York is

watch her to-morrow . . . courageous, colourful, laughing

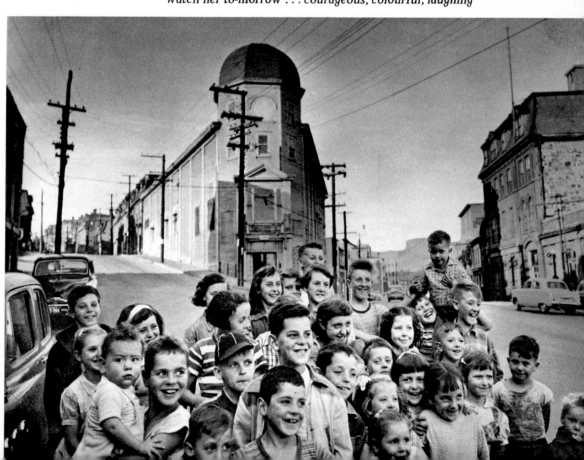

big city seemed, without reason or rhyme, to squat in clusters on the rock. Around, between, in front and behind them, were the flat porches of drying fish propped with stilts and stained by wind and wave. The open boats in the little harbour below, sitting like ducks in a pond, their noses sniffing the wind, bowed with each slap of the sea. Outside, just a few yards past the shelter of rock, the old Atlantic growled and slammed in anger. Each surge of the waves on the rocks turned the water into charging white horses—wet and puffing with frustrated fury. Here the land and the sea clashed and crashed and played an ancient game; the land said, "No", the sea said, "Yes, I'll beat you yet—just give me time". The voice of the ocean was loud; it roared its coming and receded only to charge again and again. Like an advancing foe who found a traitorous sentinel, the sea sent forth its serpent of reconnaissance. The tongue of the sea sought out the weak spots and inwards it swirled and flowed around the rocks, into the little gashes and fissures it probed and withdrew in smokey white revenge. A war of attrition—the victor declared only by the referee—Father Time!

Every Newfoundlander knows the pound and peril of the sea. His highways are waterways, his floor is the ocean, his ceiling the fog. His front and back doors are the same. He leaves the front door when the hunch is right, but sometimes he must run like the pursued for the back door. Sometimes he never makes it and the radio in his front room reports: "All hands aboard the Ruby-Jean were lost". His cradle is the rocking sea.

Courage to go out there and have your face sting as though pellets of lead were fired at long range—courage to drop your little dory in a sea which, if frozen quickly, would look like the Rocky Mountains—night and day out there are like identical twins to these men of the waves when the fish are running.

Fish, fish, fish! Down on the little wharves we could see them with pitch forks throwing up the codfish from the boats to the wharf, from the wharf to the bins, from the bins to the cutting tables. Quickly and with the deftness of artists the men and women sliced, degutted and filleted the cod. Often it was a family assembly line—father, mother, son and daughter working as their forefathers had done for hundreds of years, their hands bloody from fish insides and blue with chill, their oilskin suits stained with scale and slobber. The tubs below the cutting tables were heavy with heads

6

Here the land and sea clashed and crashed
and played an ancient game;
the land said, "No",
the sea said, "Yes" . . .

8

. . . fish, fish, fish!
Down on the little wharves
we could see them . . .

and tails and bones and insides. Around these tables in the open air stood little clusters of men slowly shifting from foot to foot, their feet and legs in rubber casings, their lips like the sea itself broken with smile and toughened with thought; their teeth pried open only by the sweet steam of pipes. Only occasionally did they speak, but each comment from the strangers prompted a look to the sea. Always these men in jest or work must watch the sea. All they have, all they will ever have, must come from the perilous road on the sea. Oh yes, these fishermen in the little villages of Newfoundland have the stained hands and the gait of those who wring their living from the depths. Inland Canada knows not men like these—strong, daring, colourful—but look at their faces and you will know. Take any fisherman in Newfoundland, look at his face and you will see almost a saint-like quality—friendly, deep, philosophic and independent as a rock and as honest as daylight. Poor in dollars they are, but rich in soul.

For hundreds of years they and their forefathers in little isolated villages cut off from the outside places have been feeling the fathoms. The tragedy of Newfoundland is that for generations these men have given their strength in the hardest of human toil, and yet they have so little to show for it in material comfort and gain. To fish is to gamble, for always in fishing there are the unannounced visitors of wind, wave, current—always the variables of good catch, poor catch, no catch; always the unknowns of foreign competition, currency devaluation, revolutions in foreign lands. Even the price of meat hits the fisherman back in Newfoundland. The question of freezing, market fluctuations, the long hauls to big cities, the ignorance of the fish handler, the ignorance of the consumer, the prejudices against fish, the number of Holy Days, all these and a hundred other things determine the price of fish down on the wharf. A sudden storm which smashes the boats to pulp, a governmental decree in Portugal, a scarcity of bait—all these may drive the price per pound down a half cent, but half a cent to these fishing people is the difference between getting by or not.

All these things have shaped the personality of the Newfoundland fishermen, have made them rugged and religious. The schooner captains never fish on Sunday, but on that day seek shelter and solace. On deck they read the scriptures aloud as do the shore fishermen. His teachers have always been the waves and rocks; he knows what he can and can't do, because

. . . look at their faces and you will know . . .

. . . All these things have shaped the personality of Newfoundland fishermen, made them rugged and religious

Nature taught him. The very power of the sea and the punishing lash of storm has instilled in him simplicity and dignity.

He knows that behind those stormy clouds is a hand bigger than man's, he knows that the riches of Rockefeller would never save him out there when the Great Hand wills the winds. Simple, hard lessons from the Master make him God fearing and humble. Countless times have the little people of Newfoundland lifted their eyes to God and asked for guidance. Nearly every Newfoundland fisherman can quote from the scriptures. These are the true Newfoundlanders with a democracy tragic in its beauty. They share profit and peril, and one man down means a whole community is up. A widow of wave and wind is never allowed to whine and waste, because the word "united" is not simply an unctuous utterance of the uplifted in the high places, but a creed which is common and chosen among the humble, low beside the sea.

Long before union with Canada, the Newfoundlander had traded with the United States, with Canada, with Britain, with Portugal, Italy, West Indies, South America, Spain. Her skippers roamed the North Atlantic and South, too. Clothes and possessions alike of these Island people showed this. From their Island perch they could look at Britain—many of the wealthier were educated there, but they never became Englishmen. Some were educated in the United States, but they never became Americans. Some were educated on the mainland of Canada, but they were not Canadians—they were Newfoundlanders.

On the mainland of Canada we are proud of being American and British—but the Newfoundlander has three dimensions. For centuries he has looked at us, too. He will forever be a Newfoundlander first, but for that matter so will a Quebecer, a British Columbian, a Nova Scotian, and it is rightly so.

Now, many Canadians seem to think that we acquired a liability when Newfoundland joined us. That is the talk of ignorant small people who do not know. Newfoundland is a prize—Newfoundland is rich in the tangibles of resources and the wonderful intangibles of character. Newfoundland is a big province—it is number seven in size—immensely rich in trees, minerals, waterpower and fisheries. Some of the world's great virgin stands of timber are here. The Hamilton River has a waterfall twice the height of

*Newfoundland is a prize—
rich in the tangibles of resources
and the wonderful intangibles
of character . . .*

Niagara and enough waterpower potential to equal most of the developed rivers of the whole of Canada. The salmon streams, the pulp mills are known around the Globe. The iron ore which drives the steel mills of Nova Scotia comes from Newfoundland, indeed every box car and passenger car in Canada runs on axles made from steel which came from Newfoundland ore. The industrial dreams of this island tide water province are enormous. Newfoundland is slowly changing from a fishery province to one of industrial prominence. Watch her tomorrow. One of the tragedies of Canada is we don't know Newfoundland. We have a cod fish mentality about her. That's why she is turning to German and European financiers for risk capital. But, oh, the intangibles of Newfoundland are fabulous. It is a tourist paradise. Each cove and community has preserved its ways, speech, mannerisms, characters—cut off and alone for so long, these island people have the smell of the sea in their nostrils; these folk in a rugged land are as soft as dew. Loyal and unafraid, courageous, colourful, laughing, nowhere will you find a more hospitable, more humorous, more humble people than in the New Found Land.

PRINCE EDWARD ISLAND

2: PRINCE EDWARD ISLAND

PRINCE EDWARD ISLAND is a vegetable garden fenced by sandy beaches and protected by salt water. Although far from the prairies it is the home of mournful cowboy laments, the horsiest place in North America, and possessing people determined to have more fun per acre than anywhere on the mainland.

Islanders are proud of being different. Some of the old timers still ask if "the foreign mail" is in, meaning the mail from across the nine-mile strait which makes them an island people. A farmer whose home faces New Brunswick once told me that he wished more foreigners, meaning Canadians, would build summer cottages on the island.

Prince Edward Island is not much bigger than a good-sized county on the mainland with a population smaller than that of London, Ontario. Yet this ocean-ringed farm has all the trimmings of the bigger provinces. Parliament is opened and closed with pomp and dignity. The Lieutenant-Governor lives graciously in a special mansion and the tiny government has the same cabinet portfolios found in rich Ontario or Quebec.

The contentment and prosperity of the island province is a monument to skill and diligence. Prince Edward Island is undoubtedly the most democratic province in Canada with very few extremes of wealth, no slums, no ugly smokestacks, no rush-hour traffic. Although the Islanders honour the pomp of statehood, Lieutenant-Governor, Premier or Cabinet Minister will be addressed by his Christian name as he strolls along the friendly streets of Charlottetown. This happy *modus vivendi* has been achieved without the wealth of a "northland", without great forest tracts, mines or power-rich rivers. It has been done by making the most of what is available.

The red soil of the island is not especially fertile, yet through diligence and research Prince Edward Island potatoes are top quality. The Malpeque oysters after decades of intense cultivation are world famous. The idea of keeping foxes in captivity was born here and the pelts command the highest prices outside. Cattle buyers come here because some of the best purebred herds in America are on the island. Even Kentucky will admit that the race horses bred on this ocean pasture have an international reputation.

The Islanders are addicted to horseracing. Harness racing is a cult and even tiny hamlets have the familiar half-mile track. From June to September the thud of hooves vies with the pound of the seas. Charlottetown, the capital, has one of the best lighted tracks for night racing found on the continent. Betting is illegal, but this does not seem to deter the sport-loving Islanders. When the Old Home Week is held in August almost the entire population heads for Charlottetown and the ranks are swelled by homesick Islanders from Boston, New York, Montreal, and Toronto. The car-ferries which transport the automobiles across the Northumberland Straits are full to the gunwales, and everyone is out for a good time.

Prince Edward Island is one of North America's last accessible but unspoiled vacation lands. Even the approaches to it are unique. Standing on deck of the big car ferry, the visitor will first be impressed by the red soil, the red banks, the great sweeps of sandy beaches, and the ubiquitous lobster traps. The next impression will be the neatness of the farms and the gentle roll to the land, but no matter where the visitors drive they will never be more than a few rods from the sea. The Micmac Indians called the island "Abegwait—the home cradled on the waves". Micmac legend has it that P.E.I.'s red soil was due to Glooscap, the great demi-god, who wanted some place to retire, so he painted the island red with a fairy paint brush.

No Prince Edward Islander ever seems to be in a hurry and he'll take a very briny squint at anyone who tries to see everything in one day. At first he might seem downright disinterested, but give him a chance to talk and he'll open up like an oyster in the steam pot. He lives on an island where family names mean something, where pride is as deep as the top soil which feeds it. He feels that you have come to his island home because it's different, because you wanted to escape the summer heat, the congestion of big cities and because P.E.I. has the warmest salt water north of New York and the best beaches anywhere. He'll fill you with boasts. He'll tell you that Canada started here and you can see for yourself the Confederation Chambers where the first fathers of Confederation met in 1864. He'll tell you that the

first automobile in North America was driven at Rustico, P.E.I. in 1866 and show you the report in the press to confirm it.

Another boast of the Islander is in citing the names of famous sons— the boys from the farms and coves who went "abroad" to run the banks, universities, industries of the continent. The list is a formidable one and it ranges from Cardinal McGuigan, Archbishop of Toronto, to John Bohlen, Lieutenant-Governor of Alberta, with scores of prominent citizens in the United States. The list is a tribute to the stability of rural upbringing combined with a sense of values in a changing world. A dollar is made to go further in P.E.I. and still retains some value. Because the very theme of the island is quality, it is no accident that potato seed from this red sandy soil sells in thirty of the fifty states.

Emigration of native sons and daughters is part of the process of education in a province 140 miles long, 4 to 40 miles wide. It cannot support comfortably more than 100,000 people, so there are more island born heads of families found in the U.S.A. than in P.E.I. Tourists come and are captivated and return, but very few immigrants ever select this province as their new home. The foreign born population is less than 1 per cent, whereas the native born is 96 per cent. The 3 per cent is what the Islanders call "Canadian" born.

The Scots represent 37 per cent of the population, English 25 per cent, Irish 20 per cent and Acadian 15 per cent. Many of the Acadian familes are descendants of those who escaped the Expulsion of the Acadians in 1755. A gentle people trying hard to hold on to their ways in an English-speaking continent, they live principally in the Rustico country on the north shore.

The north shore faces the broad Gulf of St. Lawrence and the sea sweeps upon the coast with a thundering roll. Challenging the churning surf is the delight of the tourist. The sea water is warmed by the miles of sandy beaches and swimming here is undoubtedly the most pleasant in the northern half of the Atlantic. One of our better National Parks—Prince Edward Island National Park—has miles of sand dunes and beaches to halt the breakers. Parks authorities have included the *Anne of Green Gables* house in this property and tourists who have read Lucy Maud Montgomery's enchanting stories can visit her fairy tale haunts.

Each year more and more visitors find summer delights on this long shoulder of sand dune and tumbling sea. Holidayers are intrigued by the

*Through diligence and research
Prince Edward Island potatoes
are top quality . . .*

The Islanders are addicted to horse-racing . . .

No Prince Edward Islander is ever in a hurry . . . but give him a chance to talk . . .

. . . where pride is as deep as the topsoil that feeds it

quiet charm of the place and the great sweeps of beaches speckled with so few people. There are no maddening Coney Island elbows to jab one's ribs. The visitor can stroll in his bare feet for miles and wander off into the shallow ocean water. The island's beaches hold the answer to a mother's prayer, for the children can romp in safety, build castles in the sand, poke sticks into jelly fish and cover father from neck to toe with sand. When the sun falls slowly into the sea it is fitting to end the day with a family picnic on the beach, to build your own fire and boil the lobsters which came from the very waters which made you king for a day. Prince Edward Island National Park has excellent camping facilities and each year more cottages and resorts are added to the summer estate of "the home cradled on the waves".

Prince Edward Island is refreshingly different because it is so restful. Here you are truly far from the madding crowds. The atmosphere is rural for there are no large cities. Charlottetown, the capital, has a population of approximately 15,000, while Summerside, the only other large community, claims 5,000 souls.

The Islanders seem to operate on the principle that a visitor is guilty until he proves himself innocent, but this attitude can change quickly if the visitor shows an interest in the island kingdom. Enquire and they might tell you the secrets of the oyster and how it can change conveniently from male to female. Ask and you might be shown the snuff box which belonged to Marie Antoinette or the house which was built to protect its owner against the return of the Great Flood of biblical times. So convinced was he of another flood that the roof of his house was hinged and could be raised for the launching of boats. Be sure and see one of the last remaining fox ranches and go down to the sea shore and help gather the Irish moss. If your sea legs are strong, perhaps you would like to sail with the lobster fishermen and have the thrill of pulling in these green tinged crustaceans from the ocean floor.

Whether you go to Prince Edward Island to escape from hay fever or crowds, you'll wonder why the radio stations play so many mournful cowboy laments and old time music. The answer, and what other could there be, is that Islanders like them.

NOVA SCOTIA

3: NOVA SCOTIA

NOVA SCOTIA is saved from being an island by a tiny neck of stubborn land which ties her to New Brunswick. Even if this neck were severed, Nova Scotia would not drift away, because in her mood and ways she has always been an island.

The sea at her portals—whether it be the warm waters of Northumberland, the gnawing swells of the Atlantic or the heaving tides of Fundy—has shaped her character and her destiny. Long before Columbus sailed west, Europeans were fishing the waters off Nova Scotia. The pirates and privateers knew the cover of her coves. Her first citizens lived from and traded on the sea. Even the map of Nova Scotia has marine contours—for does it not look like a giant lobster with Cape Breton as the claw?

The imprint of the European is strong here, for in one sense Nova Scotia is the most cosmopolitan of the provinces. The French, Germans, English, New Englanders, Scots, Loyalists all came in from the open sea. The first to record his stay was the Father of Canada, Samuel de Champlain, who founded Port Royal in 1605 to make it the first permanent settlement on the continent north of St. Augustine. Champlain knew Nova Scotia before he ventured further inland to found Quebec and explore Ontario. Nova Scotians are not likely to let other Canadians forget this fact. Champlain's stay in Port Royal gave the Nova Scotians a list of "firsts" in Canada—from the first play, farm, shipyard, baptism, water mill to the first social club. The English added to the list—first newspaper, first Anglican church, first Presbyterian church and the first court to administer the English Common Law within what is now Canada. To this the Nova Scotians add the names of Cornwallis, Wolfe, Nelson, Howe, Sam Slick, Evangeline, Samuel Cunard of steamship fame, and McCurdy, pilot of the first flight in the British Empire.

The sea and history are mentioned only because they have such a bearing on Nova Scotia today. The quiet, rather than fierce pride; the friendliness; the suspicion of "outsiders"; and the sour feeling that when Ottawa was Bytown, Nova Scotia skippers were sailing the seas—all these are part of the peninsular personality. After all, in the first 100 years of the white men, Nova Scotia changed hands no less than ten times. No part of Canada is more rich in adventure, romance, tradition and memories.

Visitors to this Atlantic land should remember that it is divided into four parts—Cape Breton, the Scottish lands along Northumberland, the Atlantic shore, and the Annapolis Valley, each possessing its own personality. The apple grower in Annapolis, surrounded by gracious hills and living in a bower of perfume and blossom, would scarcely understand the quick tongue of the miner who has just emerged from the deepest coal mine in the world in Cape Breton. The lilting Gaelic of the Highland Scot farmer from Antigonish would be heard in sharp contrast to the low and slow German intonations of a Lunenburg fisherman along the Atlantic. Even in speech, Nova Scotia has an interesting variety. In speech one can sense the drama of her history and the impact of successive waves of immigration. Again it is the ocean which has produced these ethnic pockets since it is the tourniquet of the ocean which has confined the differing speech to the original areas of settlement. The Lunenburger has never forgotten the German influence in his speech. The Scots in Cape Breton, Pictou, Guysboro and Antigonish have the sing-song of the Gaelic. Pure Gaelic is still spoken in Cape Breton where, in summer, the Gaelic college opens its doors. The Acadians with their warm accented English have their own regions. Nova Scotia is an interesting mixture of German, Scottish, French, American and English influence.

The lobster-shaped province is a natural playground for tourists. There is a little bit of something for everyone, and indeed no place in the whole of North America can offer as many contrasts as Nova Scotia, simply because it is old, sea girt and proud. In Halifax one can drive over the magnificent harbour suspension bridge and peer into the very funnels of Her Majesty's Royal Canadian Navy ships, or from the top of a misty hill one can look at the forest of spars in the swordfishing fleet of Ingonish, Cape Breton. The ox is still used as a beast of burden on the rock-rimmed farms of the mainland, yet tourists can also stand in wonder at aeronautical inventions in the Alexander Graham Bell Museum in Baddeck. Peggy's Cove cannot find one blade of grass on her rocky terrain, yet near Amherst is the world's largest

. . . it is old, sea-girt and proud . . . the storied city of Halifax

31

hayfield, a hayfield reclaimed from the sea and guarded by hundreds of miles of dykes, which run all round the Bay of Fundy shore. The tide goes out so far that the fishermen can drive wagons out to their nets and tourists can see the strange sight of fish hanging from nets 30 feet in the sky.

The most spectacular entry to Nova Scotia is the way Champlain came —through the gut of Digby and then into the majestic Annapolis Basin. You, too, will gasp as the boat from Saint John, New Brunswick, brings you through that narrow entrance. Now the mean tides of Fundy are behind, the waters of Annapolis shimmer in the sunlight, and the hills around beckon the traveller. South from Digby you pass through village after village of the French Acadians—unspoiled, friendly. Go the other way and you will be in the famous Land of Evangeline. This is the birthplace of the continent and one of its most charming corners. Up past Port Royal, where Champlain came in 1605, on both sides of the narrow highway the orchards stretch and run with the hills. You can almost reach the apples from the car window.

The Annapolis Valley is the name given to the fruitlands of Nova Scotia, although there are several valleys in the same area. "The Valley", as Nova Scotians call it, was taken over by New Englanders after the expulsion of the Acadians. The traveller needs no history book as a reminder because the homes, churches, town centres and buildings generally look as if they had been picked up in Vermont and gently scattered throughout the Valley. It is the most New England part of Canada, even to the church spires, shutters, white paint and the very tempo of the people. It is ironical that it was Longfellow, a New Englander, who became its greatest booster, although he never set foot in Evangeline's land. Had he done so, he would never have used those words "forest primeval".

Annapolis has not only the spell of history and romance to endear her to visitors, but she has carried on a strange love affair with the sea—a bashful one. Annapolis would not produce one Gravenstein or plum, if it were not for the mighty wall which protects her from the cold and furious winds of the Bay of Fundy. It can be sunny and hot in the orchard and yet not more than ten minutes drive away on the Fundy shore, the weather might be foggy and so cold you would need a coat. Quick contrasts in the Valley country and yet the sea is part of orchard life. There are holes in the sea-wall and the tidal rivers, with their cocoa-coloured waters, snake their way through

32

. . . the low and slow
German intonations
of a Lunenburg fisherman
along the Atlantic

33

the orchards. To keep the salt tongue from licking the roots of apple trees, dykes follow the contours of the rivers and creeks. Dykes covered with waving grass, cocoa-stained river banks, pink blossoms in the spring, the aroma of flowers with the sickening sweetness seasoned by the salty tang of the sea, what a setting is Annapolis. Add to this, Indian legends, amethysts on the beaches, oxen in the orchards and the tale of Evangeline and one can understand the charm of Annapolis.

Across the wooded spine of Nova Scotia—straight across from the Annapolis Valley—is the Atlantic side or South Shore. Gone are the soothing orchards, for now the vistas are as wide as the Atlantic. The coast is saw-toothed and one mass of scattered granite. The harbours are truly havens from the ceaseless wars between tide and rock. This is what the Nova Scotians call "true bluenose land". Some claim the term bluenose came from the bluish colour of the rocks or potatoes near Lunenburg, while others maintain it refers to the cold Atlantic and the blue noses of the fishermen.

The capital of Bluenose land is Lunenburg, the last continental refuge of the schooner. Sailing days are over, but when the ships are in the masts crowd the harbour like trees in a forest. Lunenburg is torn out of a picture of some Hanseatic town—her streets are tiered parallel to the harbour—steep and crowned, the portly old mansions equipped with widow's walks and attics. Lunenburg is a fisherman's town and the smell on a late afternoon proclaims to all noses her title. The sound of her winches and the energetic growl of auxiliary engines tell us that harvesting wealth from the Grand Banks is no job for the indolent. Lunenburgers have inherited the drive of their German ancestors who settled these rocky shores in the middle of the eighteenth century. There is so much to see on this shore, from the ovens or large caverns worn into the sides of the rocky cliffs, shipbuilding yards, fish plants, fishing villages, pulp mill, to the place where it is believed Captain Kidd buried his treasure. Be sure and visit St. John's Church, built in 1745, whose frame was put together in Boston and taken to Lunenburg. St. Andrew's Presbyterian, built in 1770, is the oldest Presbyterian church in Canada.

The long and varied history of Nova Scotia is symbolized in the storied city of Halifax. The joy and the misery of this old port have left their marks on her very fabric. No city needs a public relations programme more than

*The joy and the misery
of this old port
have left their marks
on her very fabric . . .*

35

Halifax, because many people come here with their minds already made up about her. They have heard stories of wartime Halifax when landlords supposedly gouged the poor Upper Canadians who came here; but such an image does not do the city justice. Halifax always suffers from war and should not be judged by her martial pose. Today she has thrown off her uniform and undergone a plastic surgery which is the envy of many cities in Canada.

Halifax, if the visitor will take her slowly, is a most cultured and fetching city. Visitors are forever trying to compare Halifax with Ontario cities and this should not be done. What if there are only two traffic lights on the entire length of the main business street? When was a traffic light hailed as the beacon of progress? Halifax is fortunate that she does not need them. The ways of Nova Scotia's capital are leisurely, for, after all, she has been trading with the world and shepherding ships of war for more than 200 years. This old city, like the ocean at her gates, knows how to roll with the punches.

Stand on the Citadel and look down upon this crowded peninsula with a front and back harbour rated one of the finest in the world. Here you'll see great ocean liners, salt-stained freighters, aircraft carriers, creaky old schooners, cable ships that go out to keep the Atlantic telephone lines open and a host of little tugs and busy harbour craft. The sounds are those of a sailor's town.

Visitors could spend days walking along the cobbled streets peering into old ship chandlers' shops, talking with old salts, sitting with feet dangling over the wharf side, or just looking and transporting themselves to the days when wooden ships and iron men called this home.

Look to the west of the Citadel, and the number of parks and tree-lined streets and gracious old public buildings will appeal to your aesthetic taste. Within the boundaries of Halifax are 288 acres of public gardens and parks, miles of shaded walks, seashore drives, bridle paths, old forts, towers and picnic sites. In less than ten minutes the downtown business man can be aboard his yacht headed for the grey old Atlantic. Residents living along the posh North West arm can walk to the foot of their property and dive into the sparkling salt water. Halifax is truly an ocean playground and guardian of some very striking public buildings. Few places in Canada hold more regard for history than does this city of culture.

. . . peer into the very funnels of Her Majesty's Royal Canadian Navy ships

Halifax leads Canada in the number of universities per capita. There are five degree-granting institutions in this city of 100,000 souls. King's College is the oldest English-speaking university in Canada, while Dalhousie is famous for her graduates in law and medicine, and one of the proud boasts is of the number of brilliant sons who have gone forth to reach glittering heights. The emphasis on education is an inheritance from the Scottish tradition. Many of the college students in Halifax come from small towns and hamlets which are such a feature of Nova Scotian life; towns and villages with such distinctive Nova Scotian names as Shubenacadie, Stewiacke, Ecum Secum, Musquodoboit, Shad Bay, Peggy's Cove, Larry's River, Paradise and Eureka.

Cape Breton is the independent member of the Scotian family. Cape Bretoners, although separated from the mainland by a small strait only one mile wide, like to spin yarns about how different they are from the Nova Scotians. Like Texans, I suspect they invent many of these stories. In 1956 Cape Breton ceased to be an island, when she was joined to Nova Scotia by the world's longest earth-rock causeway. The wags claim that one of the Cape Breton pipers hired to honour the opening refused to pipe since he thought Cape Breton was getting altogether too chummy with "those mainlanders from Nova Scotia". One Cape Bretoner told me with a poker straight face that he was afraid the causeway would encourage skunks to enter the island. "Never have I seen a skunk on this island—we're free of them," he boasted. Within one year a skunk was seen on the island. The old insularity was gone.

Alexander Graham Bell fell under the spell of Cape Breton. He had roamed the world and could have chosen any spot on earth but he came to live at Baddeck, Cape Breton, where he carried on research in aviation, communications, electronics and anything else that took his fancy. The Bell Museum at Baddeck contains many of his sketches and plans. Bell is buried under a boulder, which, like his old home, looks down upon the warm salt waters of Bras D'Or—a long inlet from the sea—inviting to the bather and yachtsman. Now wealthy Americans keep elaborate summer homes here and follow the road from Baddeck which leads to the top of Cape Breton and the wild Cabot Trail.

This is highland country where the Gaelic is still spoken. Here highland

38

*. . . such empires of steel and coal
at the end of a continent*

lassies dance to the skirl of the pipes at a college whose sole purpose is to further the Gaelic language and Scottish traditions. Here the annual Mod brings the Scots from this continent and abroad. Cape Bretoners chuckle when some titled Scotsman arrives from the old country unable to speak Gaelic. In this country, where the mists hang in the valleys and the hills show their teeth to the clouds, traditions linger. Strong men, stern men, have come down from those hills, one of whom was so big his father had to raise the roof to let him in the house. This was Giant Angus MacAskill, who stood almost eight feet tall and weighed more than 400 pounds; old timers will still tell the most fabulous stories of the Giant's strength—how he was hitched beside the horses, how he could smash the bones in your hand with one squeeze, yet these same admirers of the Giant will always tell you how gentle and God-fearing he was. In the little museum at St. Ann are some of his personal effects.

Cape Breton is a delightful mixture of wild beauty, grimy industrial towns and people who believe in the dignity of the individual. Only a few miles from the misty, moody highlands with their magnificent seascapes and sandy beaches is one of Canada's most intensely developed industries. Most visitors are surprised to find such empires of steel and coal at the end of the continent. Sydney and Glace Bay are the smokestacks area of Cape Breton, and while not attractive in themselves are close to everything from swordfishing, ancient ruins, vacationland, to the port for the big car-ferry ice-breaker which links Newfoundland with mainland Canada. When in the top part of the island, be sure and arrange for a swordfishing trip, but if your sea legs are wobbly, settle for a fresh swordfish steak instead.

The Scots have dominated Cape Breton so much that the second group of people, the French Acadians, have been overlooked. Most of Cape Breton's fishermen are Acadians, descendants of the first French in North America. There are only a few family names, and they are distinct from French Canadians—proud names and proud people who are determined to carry on their ways. Cape Breton offers delightful side trips to places like Ile Madame, Arichat, or some little cove with the lobster boats bobbing in the lee of the breakwater. In Cheticamp the Acadian women have developed great talent in hooked rugs, making some of the world's biggest here. The co-operative movement from Antigonish—across the Strait of Canso—has

40

... the sound of her winches and the growl of auxiliary engines

found enthusiastic support in these Acadian hamlets. Other Acadian settlements are near Halifax, Yarmouth and Digby. However, the racial contrasts in Nova Scotia are interesting because they are mild with none of the suspicion and clash so often found between the French and English-speaking Canadians elsewhere. There is something very soothing about a visit to Nova Scotia because the dominant spirit is live and let live.

Each year Nova Scotia is host to students from the under-developed countries of the world. The citizens of Antigonish have become quite blasé about the strange costumes and tongues of the Orient, India, Pakistan, Latin America and Africa. They come to St. Francis Xavier University for adult education classes in the co-operative movement.

In the early 'thirties the priests of this small Roman Catholic college launched "an operation bootstrap" to help the depressed fishing villages of eastern Nova Scotia. The meetings were held on the wharves and in the fishing shacks. The message was practical, "Get your heads together and work together—don't wait for governments to help you". The St. Francis Xavier philosophers had studied the co-operative movements of other lands. They wanted something different for Nova Scotia. They wanted the local co-operative movement to grow out of the study clubs. So, each group of fishermen and farmers sat down and analyzed their problems.

From study clubs have come the credit union, the buyers' co-operative, producers' co-operative, and today all of them are linked with Maritime wide and continental co-operatives. By studying together, buying together, selling together, the economy and the spirit of hundreds of communities have been raised. The old monopoly of the merchant and broker has been broken. The Colombo plan, United Nations and other international agencies are sending students to Antigonish.

NEW BRUNSWICK

THE TOURIST on his first trip to New Brunswick will likely scratch his head to see if it is still there or is playing tricks on him. This province, which is almost square in shape, is full of surprises and freaks.

At Saint John (natives will explode if you spell it St.) the waterfall flows backwards twice a day; at Moncton the automobiles coast uphill; at Sackville if you jumped off the wharf you'd break your bones on dry land; around the Bay of Fundy the rivers go on strike twice a day. New Brunswick is a haunt for the "believe it or not" fraternity.

New Brunswick is full of contrasts. It started out to be a Loyalist province, yet it is almost half populated by French-speaking Canadians and is now the most bi-lingual province in Canada. If the provincial birth rate is any indication of progress, New Brunswick is ahead of Quebec and shares with Newfoundland the first place in all Canada.

To the English-speaking residents the most precious plot of land here is the one bearing a monument to the landing of the Loyalists at Market Slip, Saint John. This is as good a point as any to see this interesting old port. Saint John has an Atlantic grey look to her but for the enquiring tourist there is a wealth of interest. No city in Canada has such a sensible and delightful city heart as Saint John, straight up the hill from the Loyalist landing, the traffic flows around King Square and the old Loyalist cemetery. There is a European touch with shops surrounding the square with bands playing and people strolling. Down below in the harbour there are always sights and sounds of the sea as the fishermen cast their nets right in the harbour within sight of shoppers and beside the ocean freighters which are such a part of the city's life.

At certain tides the harbour will be partly filled with foam resembling soap suds. When the tide is out, the river St. John tumbles over the rocks into the harbour to create a normal waterfall. When the tide rises, it is stronger than the fresh water and pushes back the river and causes the

famous Reversing Falls. This wrestling match of salt and fresh is staged twice daily. City planners have placed a very attractive tourist information booth and lookout at this point.

New Brunswick is a land of rivers—sylvan and cocoa coloured. The sylvan ones flow down to the sea from the forest hinterland, whereas the cocoa-coloured ones come in from the sea at the behest of the tides. Many of New Brunswick's inland streams, such as the St. John and her tributaries, have the lazy meadow look of English rivers. The St. John flows peacefully and pushes herself into a fantastic web of lake, intervale and the pasture country of the poets. Bliss Carman and Charles G. D. Roberts both knew this soft country of the St. John, a river which rises in Quebec and Maine and ends with hesitation at the famous Reversing Falls. Fredericton, the capital city, sits cosily under her elms beside the "Rhine of America", the St. John River.

The tidal rivers of New Brunswick along the Bay of Fundy shore are just the reverse of the clean inland streams. They are always cocoa coloured —always full of silt, always moody and often relentless to obstacles. The Fundy tides are among the highest in the world. On the Petitcodiac at Moncton they are so strong that they charge across the mudflats in one frightening rolling wall. The Bay of Fundy has so much water to put into the Petitcodiac in such a short space of time, she has to pile it, and the resulting Tidal Bore is an awesome feature of this rough coastline. One moment the Petitcodiac is an insipid stream, then comes the great onslaught of water which in a few minutes creates a navigable river. The rivers around Fundy go on strike twice each day. When the tides are out, there are no rivers— nothing but serpentine gashes lined with gooey mud.

Over the centuries these silt-laden waters have left their thin deposits of soil and thus fashioned the lowlands or marshes of Tantramar. No visitor should miss a visit to these salt water prairies with mile upon mile of waving grass which, enriched over the centuries by the silt-carrying tides, are known as the world's greatest hay lands. Nothing would grow here at all if it were not for the dykes which rim the coast line and follow the contours of the tidal rivers.

This Tantramar country near Sackville and around the Bay of Fundy is sometimes called "land of the flapper". The key to life on these marshes and

. . . such a sensible and delightful city heart . . .

. . . always the sights and sounds of the sea

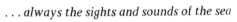

the entire economy of the area is held by the flappers. The dykes keep out the salt water but they must also allow the fresh water to find its way to the sea. Sluices, then, are pushed through the dykes with a little hinged trap door on the salt water side. When the tide rises, the pressure of salt water keeps the flapper closed; conversely, when the tide is out the pressure of the fresh water from the inside opens the flapper and drains the land.

Farmers on these lowlands are poor customers for synthetic fertilizers. Every fifty years or so, when they want to nourish the land, they open a hole in the dyke and let the sea water deposit fresh silt. Visitors will be amazed at the number of hay barns, thousands upon thousands, on these big marshes. They stand alone without trees, adjoining buildings or animal life, huge barns with lofts on either side of the doors. Before the advent of automatic hay balers, crews would go out to the marsh barns in winter and bale the hay.

Old Fundy is no mean surgeon and with the scalpel of tide and silt can change the face of the land and the commerce of towns. Sackville was once an active ocean port, shipping stoves and hay by schooner and importing the raw materials for the stove foundries. Shortly after the Federal government built a second wharf at Sackville, old Fundy rallied its forces and threw them at a key dyke. This was enough to divert the main flow of the Tantramar River. Sackville received only the backwash and within a few years, the layers of silt had shrunk the river to the size of a brook. The new wharf is now in a field.

Standing high above the barns and dykes of Tantramar are the towers of the Canadian Broadcasting Corporation's International Service. Here Radio Canada speaks to the world in a score of languages. Guides will show visitors around the maze of panels and complex equipment and let them listen to strange tongues babbling the story of Canada.

The narrow neck of land between New Brunswick and Nova Scotia also divides the waters and coast line of New Brunswick. The contrasts are sharp. On one side, the waters of the Bay of Fundy are cold, the tides are furious and the coast line gnawed and potted. A fifteen-minute journey in the direction of the Northumberland shore will offer the traveller warm water, sandy beaches and long slow tides. It can be foggy and chilly on the Fundy side of Moncton and clear and hot on the Northumberland side—only a few miles

It started out to be
a Loyalist province,
yet it is almost
half populated by
French-speaking Canadians
and is now the most
bi-lingual province
in Canada

apart. The beaches of Shediac are as good as any along the Atlantic coast.

Moncton is also home of New Brunswick's chief freak, Magnetic Hill, which seems to defy the laws of gravity. Drive your car to the foot of the hill, shut off the motor and place the gear in neutral; then sit tight and wait for the fun as your car slowly starts to roll in reverse. It gains speed as it goes back "up the Hill" reaching a speed of more than 20 miles an hour going backwards (without any help from the engine). Of course there is no magnetic pull to the earth as some imagined long ago. The conformation of the surrounding hills presents an optical illusion which makes it difficult to find the true bottom of the hill. But, whatever the reason, the experience is as good as a circus for the tourists.

Franklin Delano Roosevelt as a boy sailed the coastline of New Brunswick and became intrigued by the ceaseless urgings of the tides. His rambling old country house can still be visited on Campobello Island and the older ones on the island will spin many a yarn about the young American sailor who loved to thrust his jaw into the salt spray. It was while vacationing at Campobello that Mr. Roosevelt was stricken with polio, and for some time it looked as if the United States health authorities would deny him re-entry into his own country because of the disease. Years later, one of his first major public works programmes centred on the waters around Campobello where millions were spent in an effort to harness the tides between Maine and New Brunswick for power.

A few minutes' sail from Campobello is the cosy island of Grand Manan. There is nothing quite like Grand Manan anywhere else in North America. With the entire atmosphere timeless and relaxed, everyone has time to talk, and talk they do with a most engaging drawl almost Southern in its softness. There are no extremes of wealth and not one slum on the whole island. Property holders take a fierce pride in keeping their properties clean and painted, and rather than see a stray pebble on their highway will take turns sweeping it.

All around the island are heart-shaped weirs for catching herring. This is also sardine country and also the land of dulse. Dulse is gathered from the rocks, dried and shipped to the mainland where it is used for a variety of purposes. Grand Manan people carry wads of it in their glove compart-

ments, in their pockets, and instead of munching popcorn in the theatre, the youngsters will nibble at dulse. It is rich in iodine and the islanders boast that there has never been one case of goitre on their proud little island. You may also be served gulls eggs or wander along the rocks hunting them yourself. Periwinkles are also popular in Grand Manan. In winter, schoolboys earn handsome returns by trapping rabbits which bring premium prices in the United States where they are used to propagate the game reserves. The boys use a trap-like box to catch them and before going to school in the mornings the youngsters will tend their trap lines. The rabbit is put in a sack which is hung on a spike on the telephone pole in front of the house. The rabbit truck man will come by, collect Mr. Rabbit and leave the cash behind.

While in the south-western end of New Brunswick, visitors should visit the sardine town of Black's Harbour. Everyone in this little town is concerned with the sardine harvest and the factory which packs these silvery fish is one of the largest in the world. Nothing is wasted, even the tiny scales being collected and used by paint manufacturers. A few miles along the coast is another "biggest in the world" claim for New Brunswick. At St. Andrews-by-the-Sea is a mammoth lobster pound. Lobsters are brought here by boat and truck from all over the Maritimes where they are kept in captivity to await the dictates of the market. Conley Brothers often have more than a million pounds of live lobster at St. Andrews. Since nothing will kill a lobster as quickly as stagnant or fresh water, they are kept in pounds where the tides constantly change the water. St. Andrews also has a fisheries experimental station where scientists study the habits of these crawling crustaceans. St. Andrews is a very fashionable summer resort with many elaborate residences and a very posh C.P.R. hotel.

The Northumberland or north coast of New Brunswick, sloping gently to the sea, is tame in contrast with the Fundy shore. This, the land of Les Acadiens, is almost entirely French speaking from Nova Scotia to Quebec. The cultural heart of these friendly people is Moncton where stands their cathedral, a daily French language newspaper, French radio station and university. A few miles outside Moncton is the University of St. Joseph where instruction is given in both French and English. Many Acadian families can trace their North American ancestry back to the 17th century. In 1955 they celebrated the bi-centenary of the Expulsion of the Acadians and relatives

54

. . . in New Brunswick you'll find it

. . . this interesting old port

. . . the world's largest natural dry dock

New Brunswick is full of contrasts . . .

from Louisiana came to L'Acadie for the celebrations. All along the North-umberland coasts are little Acadian fishing hamlets and the shining silver steeples of their faith. The closer one travels toward Quebec, the more one can detect changes in the speech, since in northern New Brunswick the Quebecer has infiltrated the Acadian communities.

Edmundston on the Maine-New Brunswick border is a thriving Acadian town and New Brunswick's fourth largest city. Natives in this region jok-ingly claim they live in the Republic of Madawaska where everything is supposed to be different. Indeed it is a little triangular kingdom bordered by Quebec, Maine and the old Loyalist counties to the south. No part of the Canadian-United States border is so closely integrated as here at Edmund-ston, Madawaska county. Even the pulp and paper industry shares the border with the Canadian mill turning the raw wood into a porridge-like emulsion which is pumped over the Border and turned into paper on the U.S. side.

Lowell Thomas once wrote a book in which he said: "In New Bruns-wick you'll find it." Indeed you can—a varied list from Canada's longest covered bridge to Canada's largest military camp; from world-famous sal-mon pools to oyster beds; from little ferries toll free to wind-swept roads across the salt marshes. Salt mushrooms, quahaugs, fiddleheads, shad, gas-pereau, alewives—are but a few of the gustatorial delights of New Brunswick. One must expect the unusual in a province where the rivers are without water twice a day, where cars travel backwards and water goes uphill.

QUEBEC

5: QUEBEC

THE SHARP BOW of Percé Rock points dramatically at the great land mass of Canada which rolls from here for endless miles until the Pacific proclaims a halt. Percé is the historic and dramatic gateway to Eastern Canada and the biggest province of all—Quebec. If we allow the studied tourist quaintness of the Gaspé coast to be a prototype of La Belle Province, we do her an injustice.

La Belle Province is a delightful mixture of a tenacious clinging to custom and a thirst for change. There is no one profile of Quebec. How can there be with striptease artists in Montreal, woodcarvers on the St. Lawrence, hard rock miners in Rouyn, stout Protestant farmers in Chateauguay, cloistered nuns in Quebec City, politicians in Hull and nomadic Montagnais Indians in Ungava? The Little Lord Fauntleroys of the well-heeled English studying in a British-type boarding school at Lennoxville wouldn't know what to say to French boys at the seminary in Rimouski. The polished maître d'hôtel in a Laurentian resort has no more in common with the rollicking lumber jack of the Gatineau than men of same occupations would have in Ontario.

Not all four million people in Quebec use outdoor bake ovens or ride behind jingling sleigh bells. Any outdoor bake oven in Quebec today is staged strictly for tourists. "Les Mamans" of Quebec have changed too. They have taken to the can opener, modern packaging, radio programmes and the beautician. No province seems to have changed as much as Quebec in the last 20 years. Quebec is all dressed up in new clothes with a fancy new step but really she hasn't changed at all. That is the charm of Quebec—she only changes fashion, not style. Of the three basic loves in Quebec—church, family, land—only the latter has changed. Industrialization and the thirst created by the advertiser are the culprits in pulling people to the cities.

Quebec also has many ways of saying the same thing in the same language. The thespian on the stage of Le Théâtre du Nouveau Monde in

Montreal has almost a mid-Atlantic French accent. He has polished it and delights at the internal sounds of his own cadences. The cod fisherman a thousand miles farther east speaks the same language but one would never suspect it. Not only is there the difference between an educated and uneducated person but also between the expressions each uses. Many of the old maritime expressions of Normandy can still be heard along the salt water coast line of Quebec. The trained ear can quickly detect the differences in accent between the Montrealer and Quebec City citizens of comparable education.

Any province of such enormous geographical proportions is bound to present striking contrasts in occupation, speech and climate. Quebec is the giant of the North American continent. Its area of 594,534 square miles makes Texas blush. Quebec is larger than Texas by the addition of ten other states. To equal the area of Quebec the following American states are asked to stand: Texas, Vermont, New York, Rhode Island, Pennsylvania, Massachusetts, California, Connecticut, Maine, New Hampshire and New Jersey. There is still enough room left over for another small state. In European terms it is six times the size of the United Kingdom or the equivalent of the United Kingdom plus both Germanies, France, Italy, the Netherlands and Switzerland. La Province de Québec has three provinces and four states as neighbours.

The northern tip of Quebec on Hudson Strait is almost as far north as Dawson City in the Yukon. The difference in summer temperature between Montreal and Cape Hope's Advance is almost 30 degrees. The Quebecers who live at the point where Newfoundland and Quebec join are almost a thousand miles closer to Europe than the citizens of Hull. Quebec and Newfoundland have more salt water coast line than any other province. In Montreal, Quebec also has the title of world's busiest fresh water port. The roaring streams of her wild country give her Canada's great reserve of undeveloped water power with the Grand Falls on the Hamilton twice the height of Niagara.

The mightiest influence in the history, development and indeed personality of Quebec is the magnificent River St. Lawrence. This was the route of the brave sailors from France and England, and of the fur traders, as it is today for the steel hulls of world commerce. Along the banks of the

62

...a delightful mixture of tenacious clinging to custom and a thirst for change

tributaries, cities have grown: Hull on the Ottawa and Montreal at its confluence, Three Rivers and Shawinigan Falls on the St. Maurice, Sorel on the Richelieu, Quebec City on the St. Charles and Chicoutimi on the Saguenay. Nearly all her important towns are on either the St. Lawrence or its tributaries. The St. Lawrence cuts right through Quebec making it a province of two parts.

Actually there are many sections to Quebec. Out in the warm salt waters are the Gulf Islands. Les Isles de la Madeleine are neighbours to Prince Edward Island; Anticosti stands alone as guardian of the inland seas; then comes the Gaspé Peninsula and lower St. Lawrence with its patchwork of farms and rural ways. Here is old Quebec with the long winding main streets bending with the whim of the river, Gallic in their contours because everyone wants a verandah on the main street. In more troublous times, the building of homes close together served for protection as well. Now the farms stretch back from the river or road in long lines and with each generation they get divided with an increase in the patchwork of fences. Even in this age of the automobile, the rural Canadian wants a gallery on his house and usually a rocking chair as well.

Opposite the Gaspé Peninsula is the North Shore where only a few years ago the wilderness reigned undisturbed. Today this is the promised land and the stubborn coast line yields to the strong arm of progress. Highways are slowly moving along the rim; airlines connect the bustling towns, Canada's newest railroad—fully dieselized—roars from the St. Lawrence at Seven Islands to the moon-like wastes of Labrador.

Under the hard shell of Labrador, however, is the opposite of waste, for this is iron ore country. Millions of tons lie ready for the furnaces of the continent. British promoters are talking about fabulous power stations on the Hamilton. Some day the lamps of Toronto may be lit by energy from the foaming waters of this land which has just awakened. Prospectors comb the rocky spine for more wealth; Baie Comeau makes paper and aluminium; Havre St. Pierre ships titanium and now the big primary producers in this area are talking of keeping the mighty river open all year. Baie Comeau with its crescent-shaped streets, landscaped homes, high living standards, and bustling activity is the symbol of this new Quebec. Twenty-five years ago—nothing; today—a modern city boasting the fastest paper machines and the

64

. . . the St. Lawrence, the route for the steel hulls of world commerce

65

No province seems to have changed
as much in the last 20 years.
Quebec is all dressed up
in new clothes
with a fancy new step
but really she hasn't changed at all . . .
that is the charm of Quebec

science

66

camaraderie

religion

art

music

world's newest aluminium plant, Baie Comeau's population will soon reach a figure of 15,000.

The dividing point between the North Shore and western Quebec is the Saguenay River—one of the most spectacular and certainly the deepest river on the continent. At the top of the Saguenay is an industrial empire of pulp, paper, power and aluminium. Up this serene river come the ore carriers from South America to disgorge their cargoes of bauxite. This is aluminium country with a saga of spectacular development in the last quarter of a century. Aluminium means power and payrolls, and both are here in the Kingdom of the Saguenay. The Aluminium Company of Canada, pioneers in planned townsites for workers and families, have made this sleepy country where the story of Maria Chapdelaine was written a model of industrial progress. From here industry is punching holes in the hinterland farther north; one of them, a new mining empire at Chibougamau, already has a brand new railroad.

French-speaking Canadians call this "Le royaume du Saguenay" or Lake St. Jean country. The terrain is wild and striking and presents a startling contrast to the jet base at Bagotville, the smelters of Arvida, the spires of Chicoutimi, the pulp pile of Kenogami, the piers of Port Alfred. Canada's greatest network of power dams fans out in the country around Chicoutimi, truly a little kingdom of its own. The tempo of living, the take home pay, the patterns of leisure and even the speech mannerisms are different here. A trip up the Saguenay by boat is something no tourist should miss. The steep walls of rock and the shimmering waters themselves proclaim "le royaume du Saguenay". Besides beauty and progress this Saguenay Kingdom has the largest and tastiest blueberries on the continent; blueberries which command top prices in New York markets. This is also the haunt of l'ouananiche or land locked salmon.

Another distinct region in Quebec is the Eastern Townships to the south-east of Montreal. The English-sounding names of the towns proclaim the early settlement of this charming corner of Quebec: Granby, Waterloo, Drummondville, Sherbrooke, Warwick, Farnham, Cowansville, Victoriaville, Ascot Corner. Today, this rolling country of orchards, lakes, asbestos mines, mushroom farms and old New England type buildings is overwhelmingly French. West of the Eastern Townships is the milk shed of Montreal

Industrialization pulls the people to the cities . . .

—a pastoral belt of flat prairie and sylvan streams often known as the Chateauguay country. On the east of the Townships stretch the mining towns of the asbestos country, and the rugged hills which are part of the mining towns of the Appalachian chain give it a highland charm. For the outdoor lover this is the southern counterpart of the Laurentians and the tourist promoters here claim it has more to offer—more water, more history, more delightful towns, arable land, rolling foothills and proximity. They are looking for a name which will embrace the entire area south and east of Montreal and some wish to call it L'Estrie or Foothills or the Appalachians so that it will be recognized as a counterpart of the Laurentians.

Montrealers have an escape hatch on either side of them. They can slip north into the highly cultivated resort area of the Laurentians or they can go south in the strip of land between the river and the U.S. Border. In summer, they need to escape the heat of this our first metropolis. It will surprise many to know that Montreal, the city where the snow lingers all winter, is actually slightly warmer than Toronto in summer. Montreal's summer temperature is the same as that prevailing in Brantford, Ontario. But no matter what the season, Montreal has a personality. This, the largest officially bi-lingual city in the world, is an irresistible coquette with an intriguing mixture of old-world dashes and streamlined North American flashes.

The old and new stand gracefully together here. In another city the sight of weathered old-world shrines and sparkling skyscrapers might be labelled as garish and shocking, but in Montreal they look as if they had always been there and belonged. Students of church architecture find much to treasure in Montreal. Tourists are bound to like her for there is a little of everything here; Montreal is a metropolis, a seaport, a transportation hub, and big town for radio, theatre and television. Montreal is one of the busiest television and radio centres in the world. French TV language production totals in Montreal are greater than those of the British Broadcasting Corporation in London. The C.B.C., which employs more than 2,400 people in Quebec, claims that Montreal is the undisputed leader in French language TV anywhere—and with the two languages combined, ranks either third or fourth in the entire world. The C.B.C. cannot pipe in programmes in French so all must be produced in Montreal.

*Any province
of such enormous
geographical proportions
is bound to present
striking contrasts*

Montreal is not French as some Canadians insist. It is a Canadian city where the majority of the inhabitants speak French.

Everywhere the traveller is confronted with bilingualism. The two tongues are used on street signs, posters, restaurants; they fill the broadcast bands and even the policemen on the corners can slow one down with a torrent of instructions in either, switching from one to the other with delightful facility. The English Canadian in Montreal holds the money bags but the French-speaking citizen runs the city. Montreal is a curious workable division of authority with two cultures co-existing, with two ethnic groups working together in amity by day but going their separate ways at night. The exceptions to separate pleasures are in the fields of music and gastronomic treats for which Montreal is justly famous. The open air concerts on the mountain with the city sparkling below and the river running by are favourite nocturnal pleasures of taxpayer or traveller. The visitor in search of gustatory fancies can eat his way through the cultures of the world—Jewish, Italian, Chinese, Hungarian, American and, of course, French. For those who like good heavy French Canadian farm specialities, Montreal has them—everything from smoked pigs' feet, salt pork, blood puddings, buckwheat cakes to patates frites. The patates frites are usually sold from a gaudy, sign-plastered old automobile which manages to defy the no parking signs posted on the corner.

A generation ago, the Laurentian mountains north of Montreal were the guardians to the backward habitant farmers who dwelled there. Here was a hill-billy country of legends and ghost stories. Today the highway North has become a 70-mile street crowded with billboards and signs enticing the tourist to linger. With the exception of the coast lines of Florida no equivalent distance has been so highly developed as the Laurentians. There is something for every purse—the swish chalets with swimming pools, ski tows and curling rinks, the overcrowded lodges for the middle class, cabins for the more modest purse and, it would seem, ghastly hot dog stands and hamburger joints for anyone. It is becoming a hodge-podge despite the beauty of the land and the excellence of the better hostelries.

Maintaining mountain chalets for three months in winter is costly, so the Laurentian sales force has turned this into the valley of the four seasons. Swarms of Montrealers drive north in summer to escape the heat. Spring in

. . . those steep and winding hills between lower town and upper town

the mountains is relief from the dreary winters of Montreal and when the maple syrup is boiling who can stay away? Autumn turns the whole undulating land into hills of fire. Few places in North America can stage such a cavalcade of colour as these old hills. Sparkling white to the skier, fiery and glorious to the sightseer in autumn, such is the Laurentian valley where nearly every hamlet is named after a saint. Montreal has been blessed to have such a convenient retreat upstairs.

The time to see Quebec City is when nature has been profuse with winter trimmings and the snow sticks to the slate roofs like dobs of eiderdown. The soul of a man must be sick with grief not to be stirred by the sights of this gracious old capital. She beguiles the visitor with her twists and turns, fascinates with her sweeping panorama, intrigues with her blend of old and new and frightens with her horn honkers and spinning wheels.

If you can drive a car in Quebec in winter and escape uninjured or unintimidated, then you should be entitled to drive anywhere in North America without further driving tests. How the cars ever navigate those steep and winding hills between lower town and upper is one of the wonders of the New World. It would seem that the perpetual horn honking is meant to reach the ears of the travellers' patron saint—St. Christopher. The risks and adventures of driving in summer are only slightly less than in winter. But this is Quebec City and it is all part of the show. There is no other city even remotely resembling Quebec City, indeed the only thing in common with Montreal is the St. Lawrence River, and Quebecers will sagely point out that it looks like a river at this point.

Even the dwindling coterie of proud old English-speaking families who live in splendid array on the Big Rock are sentimental about Quebec City. They, too, have the grace and pace of this, the mother city of Canada. Along with their French-speaking citizens they regard the bigger cities of Montreal and Toronto with a very cagey eye. The brashness, the passion for tearing down and building in straight lines, the eternal rush of the big cities has no place in the heart of Quebec City. Let these crazy Montrealers and Torontonians run, run, run if they wish, but here in Quebec City we live our own way. That is the feeling, for Quebec City (save for the ubiquitous horn sounder) is softer and slower and more quiet. This proud city, whose every stone reveals a patch of Canada's history, has justly been called an historical

74

hyphen. Canada's history really started here and the traveller who does not stop to study and enquire is missing a unique attraction. Quebec City has been lavishly showered with gifts from nature, history and wide horizons for tomorrow. It is the capital of a province fairly seething with development, so the men with blueprints and financial credentials who go forth to the wilderness come first to the capital city. Many names she has; Gibraltar of America, Sentinel of the St. Lawrence, Walled City, Fortress.

Is there a view from any metropolitan heart in North America as sweeping in majestic proportions or as significant in history as that from the Board Walk in front of the Château Frontenac? Higher still on the Citadel it is even more panoramic. Looking down from The Rock to the noble basin of the St. Lawrence and far away to the purple hills, the tourists know why the earlier visitors stopped here; stopped, rested and started out again, for this was the cradle. Quebec was home to the most dazzling lists of "Greats" the New World ever entertained. As their names are called, the chapters of history respond: Cartier, Champlain, Laval, Frontenac, La Salle, Marquette, Joliette, Vérandrye, Bréboeuf, Lallemant, Montcalm, Wolfe, Lévis, Montgomery, Arnold, Carleton, Elgin, Fraser, MacKenzie and legions of others who helped bring large sections of North America into the family of civilization.

Is it any wonder the incumbents of The Rock have their own ways? Where else can the tourist in one glance fill his inner eye with such grandeur, his brain with so much history, his stomach with such delights, his heart with such dramatic and poetic portions and still be so well housed as in Quebec City? Neither poet nor painter can tell its story completely.

ONTARIO

6: ONTARIO

ONTARIO is the wealthy member of the Canadian family. It is the empire province of Canada in the same way as the State of New York is the empire state of the United States, only more so—much more so. It has the richest farmland and market, the largest industrial plant, vast forests, minerals, electric power, inland waterways and a productive unit that turns out two-fifths of all goods produced in Canada.

Ontario is the heartland of Canada, historically and geographically. It is the bridge between the eastern provinces and the western. There are four provinces on one side and five on the other. The big slice of the Canadian market is here and no wonder, for more than 32 per cent of all Canadians live in Ontario with a population close to six million. In per capita wealth and per capita productivity she has no peer; she is the workshop of the nation.

The empire province, because of her unique position and wealth, is also the leader of the family. Toronto has become the thought moulder of the nation and the keeper of the purse strings for industry. Most of the publishing houses and national radio and television production units call Toronto home. The phenomenal growth of the oil and mining industry throughout Canada is fed from money raised in Toronto. Each year great numbers of young Canadians come to Ontario to fulfil their ambitions.

Location and physical structure give this banner province her market, her raw materials, her hydro-electric power and her low cost transportation. What Ontario lacks in raw materials, her neighbours have. There is no coal in Ontario but Pennsylvania is just across the lakes. The iron ore of Minnesota is not far away, and oil and gas are piped in from the prairies.

Toronto is only an overnight trip to most of the big cities of the United States. The populous belt of the United States is just next door and provides both a source of and market for Ontario's raw materials. Four of the five

Great Lakes form her southern boundary. The St. Lawrence River links her with the Atlantic Ocean. Some day soon the province will have a salt water port of her own on the Atlantic Ocean at Moosonee, James Bay.

The province has many regions—north-western, north-eastern, eastern, Lake Ontario, Niagara, Georgian Bay, mid-western, south-western and metropolitan. These nine regions can be roughly grouped into two divisions: old southern Ontario and northern Ontario, with the Pre-Cambrian Shield as the dividing line. Rocks, lakes and forests stretch a thousand miles to the tundra of the north and to the prairies on the west. Below, it is part of the interior plains of the continent with fertile land and temperate climate and with more than 90 per cent of all Ontarians living here.

The two divisions are unequal by almost every test. The north is seven times as big as the south. The north is the treasure chest which feeds the south and exports to the world. From this "resourceland" come the raw materials—minerals, forest products, water-power, fish and fur. Whether it is gold, nickel, uranium, copper, platinum, iron ore, newsprint or beaver pelts, northern Ontario has it. The southern part, crowded and busy, is the farmland, workshop and metropolitan heart of the province. The factories produce a range from automobiles, aircraft, chemicals, agricultural implements to drugs, books, textiles and foodstuffs.

The range of climate is just as spectacular. The "southerner" in Niagara Falls shudders when he learns that the temperature in White River is 50 below zero. Such temperatures are unknown to him, and indeed he complains when the thermometer drops to 20 above. The distance from southern Ontario to the northern limits is 1,050 miles; the latitude ranges from 41°41' at Lake Erie to 56°50' at the most northerly point in the province. In more graphic terms this means Ontario ranges from peach farms in the south to igloos in the north.

When I first came to Ontario, I was most impressed by the rich fat look of the farms. I came from a part of maritime Canada where many farms were scrubby and marginal, and where the farmers generally indulged in cagey trading to survive. Not so in most of old Ontario's farm belt. The large stone houses with their triple stories and solid grey look impressed me. The barns were big, and machinery seemed to be scattered all over the place. The silos looked fat and so did the cattle. The farmers looked more like

*The north is
the treasure chest
which feeds
the south
and exports
to the world*

businessmen, and their sons and daughters went to college—so it seemed to me on the first visit.

The backbone of Ontario is the farm belt. From the border of Quebec to the shores of Georgian Bay is as good an example of mixed farming as one can find anywhere. Agriculture follows manufacturing as Ontario's second industry. With more than 70 per cent of Ontario's population being urban, the farmer has a ready home market, and, in addition, he exports farm products to the United States.

Farming in southern Ontario is highly mechanized, highly commercialized, and often highly specialized. Niagara yields peaches, pears, plums, grapes, apples, strawberries and market vegetables. The Lake Ontario region east of Toronto is famous for dairy products, cheese and fruit. West of Toronto, the area produces livestock, tobacco, tomatoes, cheese, sugar beets, onions, corn and a great variety of garden produce. Ontario is the world's greatest shipper of pure bred cattle, and transports many of them by air to the United States and Latin America.

With the exception of tropical fruits, it is possible to grow almost anything in Ontario. Ontario is closer to self-sufficiency in food than most parts of North America. Ontario makes Canada almost 100 per cent self-sufficient in cigarette tobacco. Ontario cigarette tobacco is exported to Europe. The province also produces more wine than any area in North America with the exception of California. The most southerly tip of Ontario is on the same line of latitude as the northern line of California or the French Riviera. The southern tongue of Ontario which juts into the United States is jokingly called "the banana belt" or the "sun parlour of Canada".

Ontario has a delightful and efficient blend of farm and factory. Many of the so-called farmers' towns have a high and steady payroll from industry. Ontario has dozens of these solid, tree-lined old towns surrounded by rich farms with the factories hidden but always there. The unionized factory worker, the retired farmer and the local merchant may not integrate too well socially but they have not changed the face of these old towns. The neon lights flash on the main street, the beer parlours are noisy and overcrowded, but on the side streets the stately old homes stand timeless and serene. There is plenty of inherited wealth in those old mansions, wealth from factory and farm alike.

. . . fishermen come by the thousands

Westerners who come to Ontario are always impressed by the trees of this southern belt and by the solid face of the business districts and homes. Southern Ontario towns with the vested look of time and wealth represent the real backbone of Ontario. In politics and influence this is Ontario. Toronto may have the glamour, but it is the small cities and towns of Ontario which provide the market and the political impact. There are so many of them—Stratford, Guelph, Galt, Brantford, Chatham, St. Thomas, Woodstock, St. Mary's, Owen Sound, Port Hope, Cobourg, Trenton, Brockville, Belleville, Perth, Orillia, Midland, and Lindsay. These are but a few and we have not mentioned the junior cities—Kitchener, Peterborough, Cornwall, Oshawa, St. Catharines, and Niagara Falls. In the bigger league are Ottawa, Hamilton, Windsor, and London.

Ottawa as the nerve centre of Canada has the majesty of a capital city and the mediocrity of a traders' town. Queen Victoria picked a noble setting for our capital city on the banks of the Ottawa River, noble and symbolic because the river cuts a clean line between the wild hinterland and the settled farmland. The Ottawa River also draws an ethnic line between Anglo-Saxon and Latin. On one side old Quebec stands back to flirt but solid Ontario is not too sure. At this one point the two titans of Canada face each other.

The green copper spires of this turreted town dominate the trade routes of explorer and voyager and the leap-frogging hills of the Pre-Cambrian Shield. The builders of Canada knew this Ottawa portage as the first of the trans-Canada highways. Ottawa is so expressive of big, raw, outdoors Canada. Our wealth comes mostly from the rock, water and forest, and the turrets of Parliament Hill look down upon this trinity of resources. Within the shadow of the Peace Tower of Parliament, the waters still froth and tumble and the logs assemble in jams. The wilderness on the north side still speaks at the gates of our capital.

On the south side of the Ottawa River, the whole mood and tempo of the land changes; the streams are lazy and the land is more pastoral. The wild hills have gone. Even the towns and villages have a different look. The one-street villages so common on the Quebec side of the river give way to the grid street pattern of old Ontario. Ottawa, the capital, straddles the two worlds of Canada.

84

It has the richest farmland and market,
the largest industrial plant,
vast forests, minerals,
electric power, inland waterways
and a productive unit
that turns out two-fifths of all the goods
produced in Canada

There is something of all Canada in her profile. The granite finger of Parliament's towers thrusting into the sky is symbolic of a new, clean country; rich and hopeful for a better world. The loneliness of the prairies, the symmetry of the forests, the vigil of the coasts are somehow expressed in this Peace Tower. No Canadian can lift his eye at this tower and stand unmoved.

London, almost exactly half-way between Toronto and Windsor, is the dowager city of Ontario. It is the "capital" of south-western Ontario—the rich farm-factory belt between lakes Ontario and Georgian Bay. More than any other city it expresses the spirit of old Loyalist Ontario and the new surging industrial tomorrow. Each year London is ringed by new industries and suburban developments, but still the city keeps a solid gait and does not change her face. The hot rod enthusiasts and motorcycle brigades shake Dundas Street with noise, but the old and proper families will run for arms if anyone suggests disturbing a landmark tree. London is said to be the richest city in Canada, and the old guard has no plans for abandoning the title. Farm, factory, old family and university blend delightfully in London.

Windsor is the fourth largest city in Ontario. In tempo, temperament and take-home pay, it is in a class by itself. Windsor is a box seat city. The Windsorite is a good Canadian but he lives so much under the shadow of Detroit that he is orientated that way. A citizen of Windsor receives his pay and pays his taxes in Canada, but when he wants to play Detroit is the playground. The skyscrapers of Detroit form a constant backdrop to the main street of Windsor. The shops, night spots and sports arenas wink at him every day and night.

Windsor has more opportunity to see big league baseball, hockey, football, and prize fights than any other Canadian city. Citizens of Windsor live much closer to downtown Detroit than citizens of Detroit do, because downtown Detroit is just the other side of the tunnel. Windsor is the gateway of the busiest border crossing point on the United States-Canadian line and is the symbol of Ontario's close ties with the U.S.A., but that same Windsor is proudly Canadian and a rich contributor to our economy.

Nearly every Canadian writer and many itinerant journalists have tried to put Toronto into words. Salesmen in their trips across Canada have always been conscious of a sales resistance the moment Toronto is

Toronto is only an overnight trip to most of the big cities in the United States 89

mentioned. Tugging at Toronto's coat-tails is almost a national game, even though many of those who chide Toronto for her blue laws come from Canadian cities whose Sunday quiet would make Toronto seem riotously noisy.

The strange twist about this Toronto-baiting from within Ontario and from other provinces is that secretly these Canadians are proud of Toronto. The very man from Regina who chides Toronto when at home will sing her praises when abroad. Many times I have heard eastern Canadians, and even Montrealers, trying to tell Americans what a modern city Toronto is with the world-famous exhibition, Royal Winter Fair, Sportsmen's Show, subway and Maple Leaf Gardens.

The rich booming Toronto of today with its night clubs, bars, jazz festivals, horse races and its ball games on Sundays, bears no resemblance to the old Toronto the Good. Toronto has grown up. It is metropolitan and cosmopolitan. This city of 1,500,000 souls seems to have developed a speciality of doing things well and in a big way.

Toronto is the model for metropolitan government throughout North America, and nearly all big cities on the continent send representatives here to study the system. Toronto's transportation has long been the envy of most North American systems. Her publicly owned exhibition plant is not only the finest in North America, but also the biggest. The elaborate permanent plant gives Toronto a host of attractions such as the Royal Winter Fair and Canadian National Sportsmen's Show, both of which are the largest in North America.

Since the end of World War II more than 400,000 new Canadians have settled in the Toronto area. This impact of almost a quarter of the population bringing their own ways can be seen in the many European restaurants and shops established in Toronto. Between Spadina Avenue and Bathurst Street the tongues of Europe babble among the bazaar-like stalls which crowd the sidewalks. Foreign language papers are sold and merchandise hawked from the streets.

Toronto is a well run, rich city. It has more cars per capita, more money and more of most things than any big city in Canada. It is the busiest financial centre in Canada and in share volume its stock exchange frequently out-sells the Wall Street exchanges. Prospectors probing the rocks of

art

music

science

sport

Ungava, the Yukon or Nova Scotia likely found their grub-stake in Toronto. Even the big mining boom in Quebec is largely financed through Toronto. The mining communities of Val d'Or, Rouyn, Noranda in Quebec are supplied mostly by Toronto wholesale firms.

The whole of southern Ontario enjoys a high standard of living. It would not be so high in terms of income or leisure if it were not for the treasures in the attic. The Ontario northland not only produces much of the wealth but also provides the playground for the south. The northland makes Ontario Canada's leading producer of minerals, second in pulp and paper, first in fur and one of the world's biggest users of hydro-electric energy. From this heavily forested and rocky northland comes 85 per cent of the Free World's supply of nickel and almost half of Canada's copper. It is also the world's largest supplier of platinum and yields a host of industrial minerals. It holds most of Canada's gold mines and the Algoma district on the north shore of Lake Huron has one of the biggest uranium camps in the world. Power from rocks, power from water and profit from trees—such is the great hinterland of northern Ontario.

The citizen of Kapuskasing has no more in common with his cousin in southern Ontario than a Vancouverite has with a Haligonian. The climate, topography, dress, tempo, income level and even the foliage around the northerner bear no resemblance to the south. It is another world which crawls into its own lair in winter but flings wide the doors in summer. Like swarming ants the southerners invade the green belt of the north with its countless lakes and bays. The weekend exodus fills the highways and adds more digits to the traffic toll of the nation. "Going up north" for the weekend or for the whole summer is a cult in Ontario.

In most parts of Canada people speak of "going to the cabin". In Ontario it is invariably "cottage". Each year, as highway facilities are improved, the cottage line is pushed farther north. So many cottagers have an outboard motor and boat that the call of the loon in this fantastic web of lakes has been lost in the whine of the outboard motor. It is difficult to imagine a lake in northern Ontario without the sound of the outboard, that little portable workhorse that has changed the pattern of summer pleasure.

Northern Ontario has so many lakes that it is difficult to determine whether this is land spotted with lakes or water speckled with islands.

. . . the bridge between the eastern provinces and the western

93

Ontario claims to have close to one million lakes, and that means big business, for American and southern Ontario fishermen come by the thousands. This province has some 140 kinds of fish, from the huge maskinonge to pike, black bass, pickerel, trout and even sturgeon. On the Atlantic coastline of northern Ontario there are sea fish and one of North America's feeding grounds for migratory birds.

The Ontario Northland Railroad, during the bird shooting season, runs a Blue Goose Special from North Bay to the salt water shoreline. Tourism is big business and many communities depend almost entirely on the visitor trade. Swanky hunting and fishing lodges, resorts, camps and park sites are the new features of this northern country, the playground for the rich province of Ontario. And if Ontario ever tires of dragging herself north each weekend, she can look out the front door at four of the five Great Lakes with the St. Lawrence, Niagara Falls and the Thousand Islands thrown in. Ontario is an empire province.

MANITOBA

7 : MANITOBA

THE CREE INDIANS had good reason to name the present capital of Manitoba Win-nipiy or murky water. There is no frolic to these rivers as they carry the rich prairie soil down toward the cold Atlantic seas. They act as if they did not want to get there but are sulky and sluggish and keep looking back. However, without these murky waters there would have been no Winnipeg because on their backs flowed the commerce of fur and on their banks Western settlement started.

Winnipeg might well have been called Buffalo for everything about the city and land is big. It is the Chicago of Canada, guarding and feeding the sweeping lands west of the Great Lakes. It is a broad shouldered town. The sky above her, the width of the streets, the heft of the buildings, the energy of the people all make this a most impressive gateway to the West. Even the climate in Winnipeg is dramatic.

The land, too, puts on a show and marks dramatically the line between east and west. Nature wielded a mighty knife east of Winnipeg when she cut off the rocky spine of the Pre-Cambrian shield which runs through Ontario. Where the rocks and lakes cease their game of hide and go seek, the prairie unfolds her unending delights. The traveller knows immediately that he is in another world. The prairie sweeps in a grand highway to and beyond the capital of Manitoba. Winnipeg is an island in this sea of land. From slightly west of the Ontario border the tidy dimensions of eastern Canada are lost in a great spectacle of sky and land. This is the West.

Winnipeg looks more western than many of the cities between it and the Rockies. The flatness of the land and the spacing of the heavy down-town buildings give it a big city sky line. It is an easterner's image of what a western city should be, but, to the Canadians living farther west, it is an eastern city. The Winnipeger is undisturbed by these comparisons and prospers as the gatekeeper in the middle of Canada.

Almost half the population of the Province of Manitoba lives in the

Winnipeg area, which ranks as Canada's fourth largest city with more than 400,000 inhabitants. At the turn of the century many enthusiastic Winnipegers predicted it would be the largest city in Canada. Although Winnipegers often look with suspicion on the politics of eastern Canada, they have evidently forgotten that it was Vancouver which governed their growth. When the Panama Canal was built the hinterland of Winnipeg shrank. No longer could Winnipeg pull the wealth of the entire West through her funnel. Vancouver, in the name of Panama, reached out across the Rockies and into the western fringes of Saskatchewan, so wheat could then move westward.

Winnipeg is now performing a reverse on history—it is looking north. It is a big look, for the northern boundaries of Manitoba stretch to the barren lands of the north beyond the line of trees. Manitoba, in Churchill, has the only ocean port on the prairies. Churchill is on the Atlantic Ocean, where the Hudson's Bay Company built a fort in 1685. The French and British were fighting in northern Manitoba before the close of the eighteenth century, the first Manitobans came in through the Atlantic door, and the fur traders explored the Churchill, Nelson and Hays rivers long before anyone had heard of the Red and Assiniboine far to the south. Only when the fur traders penetrated the overland routes to the east, did the history of Manitoba shift to the south and the land of murky water. Fur and wheat built their capital at the junction of the Red and Assiniboine, and the rivalries between fur traders, Indians and settlers gave southern Manitoba a stirring chapter in Canadian history.

At last Manitoba is looking north and realizing what treasures lie between the prairie and the lowlands of their Atlantic coastline. The north is a rugged country of forest, rock and water, and rolling tundra. More than 55 per cent of the province is forested and the wealth from trees and rocks and the energy from rivers is slowly eclipsing the prestige of wheat and mixed farming in the flat lands of the south. Copper, lead, zinc, nickel and a host of minerals pour out of the north. The northern rivers run wild through the hard rock and laugh at their timid cousins to the south. There is nothing murky or sluggish about these power rivers ready for the professional engineers.

The northern Manitoban has been shaped by the rugged terrain and

The east meets west at Winnipeg, and so does the north and south . . .

looks upon the residents of the capital city as effete, just in the same way that Winnipegers sometimes regard the easterner. Manitoba's frontier is no longer on the prairie. The sodbusters of the prairie have given place to a new breed of settler who lives beside the diamond drill, bulldozer, hydro dam and mining shaft. Towns no longer grow by trial and error; they are planned on draughting boards. The big mining companies are doing for Manitoba in a scientific way what the fur traders and settlers did in an age of laissez-faire.

Three out of the seven principal centres in Manitoba are beyond the prairie. Excluding St. Boniface, which is part of the Winnipeg area, Flin Flon, with a population of more than 10,000, is the third largest city in the province. The Pas is sixth and Churchill seventh. Undoubtedly, only a very small percentage of Winnipegers have ever seen these northern towns since Flin Flon is more than 400 miles by highway north of Winnipeg and Churchill, the salt water port, close to 1,000 miles beyond Winnipeg, can only be reached by rail or air.

Once a year the Canadian National Railways run an excursion special to Churchill out of Winnipeg. Not many Winnipegers are interested and most of the tourists come from the United States. The "Iceberg Special", as some refer to it, rolls through the three physical areas of Manitoba and gives an easy and pleasant view of the prairie, coniferous woodlands of rock and water, and finally the partly barren plains beyond the line of trees. This excursion is fêted in typical northern hospitality at each stop. The chambers of commerce roll out the barrel and the train itself is a hospitality wagon absorbing the friendliness of the north.

At The Pas the tourists can catch the first impression of a booming northern town. Even the air is different—clean, crisp and invigorating. Here they can inspect mementoes of the Sir John Franklin expedition, hear church services in the Cree language and rub shoulders with prospectors, Indians, trappers, lumberjacks and suave promoters out of Bay Street, Toronto. Residents of The Pas will tell them about the annual Trappers' Festival held each February when the workers of the bush and beyond celebrate a mardi gras of the snows. The muskeg itself trembles when the Trappers' Festival is in full swing. There are dog races, dances, banquets, and parties which never seem to end. On the main street, the loudspeakers proclaim the events: fish baiting and skinning contests, climbing a greased pole,

. . . the sky above her, the width of her streets, the heft of her buildings

a race through the snow for fat Indian ladies, prizes for the most luxuriant beards, games of chance and bets available to anyone on the dog races. The tourist on "Iceberg Special" is never bored with stories in The Pas.

Flin Flon is another stop on the excursion into Manitoba's north—and what a story Flin Flon has to tell. Manitoba's third largest centre didn't start producing lead, zinc, copper, gold and silver until 1927, so Flin Flon has many characters who can remember when the trails sunk deep in the muskeg. Prospectors hunting for riches gave the town its name. At an abandoned camp site in the wilderness they found a withered dime novel called *Sunless City*, which some previous and lonely prospector had left. Both the cover and the end of the story had disappeared, but this did not dim their interest in sharing the fictional story.

Sunless City featured a fabulous character, Josiah Flintabbatey Flonatin, who had descended into the core of the earth in search of riches. The Canadian prospectors shortened his name and kept referring to old "Flin Flon" and since they did not know the ending they speculated on the adventures of this fictional character from England. Sometime later when they themselves found a rich vein of copper in northern Manitoba's northland, they suggested the place be called Flin Flon. Now Flin Flon is a most progressive little city with a high standard of living. Flin Flon spent some twenty years in trying to find the name of the author and a genuine copy of the cheap paper-back novel. Finally a book-seller in England found one and *Sunless City* is now under glass as the proud possession of Flin Flon—a city where they find it cheaper to keep the street lights burning all day and more convenient to build their houses on stilts. In the early days it was too expensive to blast the rocks, so the houses were put on top of them and added to as the family grew. The sewers were laid on top of the rocks encased in wooden boxes, and these in turn became sidewalks, but such is the pace of Flin Flon who knows what is there today? Travellers on the "Iceberg Special" will never forget this city of the rocks.

The dramatic end of the C.N.R.'s excursion is Churchill. Visitors are slightly shocked to see European sailors talking to Eskimos and United States and Canadian soldiers. Churchill is home to them all for it is an Atlantic port, an Eskimo village and a strategic base for northern defence as well as a trading post and embarkation point for prospectors looking for minerals

Fur and wheat
built their capital
at the junction
of the Red
and the Assiniboine

*The Red
has made Manitoba
a cosmopolitan
province . . .*

beyond. Generals, air commodores, meteorologists, radar specialists, missile firers, Eskimos, Indians, fur traders, tourists and modern factors meet in Manitoba's most northerly town. Prairie wheat goes out and European cars, and commodities come in to this, the oldest settlement west of Quebec.

Churchill has a limited season because of the ice in Hudson Strait, but many dreamers on the prairies think that with more powerful lobbies and with radar and specially built ships it will be a major Atlantic port. Many Manitobans hope it will thrive as a tourist attraction. After all, they say, it has history, contrast, primitive peoples nearby and the attraction of the Atlantic Ocean on the rim of the prairies. It also has a most exciting sport, catching white whales. The whales come "en masse" to the harbour of Churchill. What more could a hunter wish than the excitement of an Eskimo guide and boat and the prospect of harpooning and then shooting a whale in a prairie province in the shadow of grain elevators and ships from Europe?

Manitoba's first gate was in the north. As the Key Stone province Manitoba is also dead centre for the Continent. The east meets west at Winnipeg and so does the north and south. The Peace Gardens on the Manitoba-North Dakota border slightly below Winnipeg are almost at the half-way point between the Equator and the North Pole. This prairie garden of 2,300 acres has been set aside as a memorial not only to the good neighbourhood of the United States and Canada but as proof that land, climate and sky know no fences. In the second stage of Manitoba's development, the settlers and commerce came through this American portal and accounted for the settlements in the Red River.

The Red River Valley between Winnipeg and the United States border should be known to every Canadian schoolchild. What Canadian has not heard of pemmican, Red River carts, Red River jigs, Red River Rebellion, Métis, Louis Riel, fur trade rows and fights between settler and trader? The first shipment of wheat from western Canada to the east went up the Red River to St. Paul. The first "iron horse" locomotive in western Canada came down the Red by paddle wheeler and can be seen today in the C.P.R. station in Winnipeg. Fort Gary is in every school book.

No river of its size felt so much blood and sweat in the making of Canada as did the Red River of Manitoba. The march of Canada either went up it,

. . . making sure it is the world's best

down it, or across it. It draws an ethnic line even today between the French-speaking Canadians of St. Boniface and the English-speaking Canadians of Winnipeg. John Greenleaf Whittier wrote verse about it and historians tell about it. Winnipeg was almost drowned when the Red turned white in the anger of spring. In summer the Red is languid and dirty faced, but occasionally in spring when the melting snows of Minnesota agitate her, she fumes at the ice in Lake Winnipeg farther north and spills her spleen across the prairie and into the city canyons of Winnipeg. The Red has been a portage for Canada's western march and a problem for those who inhabit her banks. Her feet are too far south and her mouth too far north. The Red starts just a few miles north of the head waters of the Mississippi River and of her 545 miles only 105 are in Manitoba.

The Red has made Manitoba a cosmopolitan province. The French Canadian followed the fur traders and voyagers to her banks and made St. Boniface the largest French-speaking community west of Quebec. The Indian and half breeds came here for the fur trade. The Scottish and English settlers established a colony here. The Icelanders came via the Red and settled in Gimli, the largest Icelandic settlement outside of Reykjavik. The Mennonites, Ukrainians, Germans, Hutterites and Central Europeans came too. In southern Manitoba not only is the old German spoken but religious books in this tongue are published and exported to Mennonite colonies throughout the world. Winnipeg itself is home to a score of ethnic groups.

Memories of these colourful days when the Red River was the highway and boundary line between east and west have been preserved in Winnipeg. The most interesting museum in the city is in the Hudson's Bay Company department store where everything from girdles to fly swatters are sold. Shoppers can leave the display racks with their modern sales gimmicks and in a few seconds slip into another age. Close your eyes and dream a bit and you can hear the screech of the Red River carts on their way west—can hear the bull whip crack and the lilting songs of the voyager. The 'Bay museum has a full-dressed Indian, a genuine Red River cart, a York freight boat and the costumes and tools of the Métis, Eskimos, trappers, traders and adventurers.

Across the Red River, the graveyard in St. Boniface holds the remains of many of the colourful founders of the West. The Roman-Byzantine

. . . the Hudson's Bay Company built a fort in 1685

Manitoba plays hard in a big playground

towers of the Basilica which Whittier called "Turrets Twain" look down upon monuments to Vérendrye, the discoverer of the plains, and Riel, the man who set the prairies ablaze. Manitoba's history can be seen, but if you want also to feel the history of the province, take the s.s. *Kenora* at Selkirk and sail down the Red to Lake Winnipeg, an inland sea which is larger than Lake Ontario. It takes a full week to make this cruise from the shadow of a big city, along historic waterways, past the old forts and into a land of genuine Hudson's Bay trading posts at Norway House. Here soft drinks, camera film and sun glasses are sold beside furs, hides, moccasins, beads and parkas. The Indian comes here to trade as his forefathers did when Norway House was founded at the end of the eighteenth century.

Manitoba is full of surprises. From off the prairies you can climb suddenly and swim in sparkling almost mountain pure water at Riding Mountain National Park. On the Delta marshes you can listen to the trumpeter swans or drown your own voice amid the chatter of geese—acres and acres of them. At Morden, the experimental farm grows cherries and prairie apples and has a most stupendous display of flowers. The sunflowers of southern Manitoba grow taller than a man's head and the refinery at Altona turns them into oil. Lynn Lake, the nickel town in the north, was picked up, put on sleds and hauled by tractors hundreds of miles farther north and then, unlike Humpty Dumpty, it was put together again.

Manitoba is a sportsman's delight whether he goes in for fishing, bird shooting, or big game hunting. The world's record for lake trout is proudly mounted and displayed in the legislative building. Men sheepishly admit that this 60-odd pounder was caught by a lady schoolteacher. The biggest trout spree in Canada is held in Flin Flon each July in a week-long festival with a most fantastic array of prizes—cars, refrigerators, television sets, trips to exotic lands, for anything goes in this exuberant land of the north. Big name bands and singers are brought in and the streets echo with summer dances, beauty queens strut, and gentlemen pit skill and strength in the festival contests. Manitoba plays hard in a big playground.

SASKATCHEWAN

8: SASKATCHEWAN

IF BY ACCIDENT a magic carpet should set a traveller down on the plains of Saskatchewan, he would immediately know that he was in Canada. Saskatchewan in many ways is more Canadian than any other part of this country and comes closer to the image, accurate or not, of a young, restless, vibrant country with oceans of land and opportunity.

The speech of the people of Saskatchewan is as clean and crisp as the skies above them. Saskatchewan people talk in a manner that all Canadians think they use. It is neutral, and untainted with the affectations more prevalent in older centres. The natives seem to look taller and more vigorous than their eastern cousins. Maybe this is all imagination, but there is something about the march of the grain elevators, the sight of mounted policemen, the fertility of the land, the violence of the climate, and the vigour of the people which makes Saskatchewan very Canadian.

Saskatchewan has been called the breadbasket of Canada and indeed she produces 60 per cent of all our wheat and occupies 40 per cent of all the cultivated land in Canada. Everyone knows she is famous for exporting wheat, but not everyone hears about the export of brains. Saskatchewan, I suspect, outshines the Maritimes in sending bright young natives to the west coast and the eastern cities. Undoubtedly Saskatchewan has produced by far more personalities for national radio, television and journalism than any other province. Toronto is full of these transplanted westerners; the federal civil service knows these bright young men from the plains, and so does many a hockey coach.

This unusual propensity to serve the entertainment, editorial and sports world of the nation gives us a clue to the life on the plains. It is the old story of self reliance and the wholesomeness of the home. The farmer must deal in big dimensions of land if he wishes to live from the sale of wheat, so the farm homes are far apart with nothing between them but the same thing—wheat, wheat and waving wheat. It is the same with the

. . . she produces sixty per cent of all our wheat

villages or small towns, they are on their own for entertainment. Saskatchewan must have the highest incidence of amateur musicians, magicians, singers and entertainers in Canada, and she undoubtedly has the most critical radio listening audience in Canada.

The climate in spring and winter adds to the problem of isolation. People just don't travel when the roads are impassable. They stay home, but when the roads are clear, the Saskatchewan citizen has no peer in Canada—he will go anywhere, anytime. Distance doesn't seem to scare him. If there is a rodeo, donkey baseball game, football match, hockey contest, or political rally, away he goes along the long straight stretches of highway, whether the distance be four or four hundred miles. With power machinery, the farmer who grows only wheat has time on his hands.

Despite the obstacles of distance and climate, the Saskatchewan citizens are the champion joiners whether it be for political meetings, tourist councils, farm conventions, study clubs, culture or sport. Saskatchewan is unquestionably one of our most politically conscious provinces. To the stranger, it seems there is an endless round of fraternal, business and political gatherings. The life in the small towns is also closely woven around the church, lodge and the ubiquitous curling rink. The revolution in farming enables the farmer to live in the small town or village where social life is most democratic. Around the curling rink all hands will join—the farmer, minister, merchant, lawyer, doctor, the railroad ticket agent and even the grader from the egg exchange.

Saskatchewan, despite its small population, has written a remarkable story in a short time. The sodbusting and homesteading days of the pioneers were only yesterday. Saskatchewan's history is vibrant and colourful because it is almost a part of today, and orators of the province never fail to pay homage to the pioneers. The Museum of Natural History in Regina which was opened during Saskatchewan's Golden Jubilee "is dedicated to the honour of all the pioneers who came from many lands to settle in this part of Canada. It stands as a tribute to their vision, toil and courage which gave so much to Saskatchewan and the nation."

The affection for the early settlers and history is very sincere in this province. Not even Quebec has worked so assiduously to preserve its history. More than 100 historic sites have been marked and reams of literature on

116

Saskatchewan's stern beginnings were produced during the jubilee celebrations when every hamlet re-enacted some historic event. The provincial tourist advisory councils are stressing that the flavour of Saskatchewan be preserved in décor, architecture and nomenclature.

The most outstanding effort at preservation of the past is in the Western Development Museums at Saskatoon, North Battleford and Yorkton. This was a most imaginative effort to gather and preserve specimens of the machinery and implements which opened up the West. These museums are both a tribute to the pioneers and a reminder of the technological revolution in farming. They have a unique collection of early farm machinery, antique cars, buggies and pioneer household equipment—hundreds of irreplaceable machines from giant steamers to primitive wooden ploughs. The advance of western civilization is easily seen in a visit to one of these fascinating museums.

The exhibits are generally donated by patriotic citizens from all over the province. When a machine is received in dilapidated condition it is restored to good working order before being placed in the museum. Once a year the museum becomes a moving exhibition called Pion-Era, which is to Saskatchewan almost what the Stampede is to Alberta. During the first week in July the museum comes to life for six days. Every piece of machinery on wheels, no matter how old, is rolled out and demonstrated to the cheering throngs. The giant steamers and straw-fed burners growl and belch as once again they fill the prairie air as they did 50 years ago. The Indians erect tepees, the Doukabour women hitch themselves to a plough and demonstrate how they helped break the prairie sod. Pion-Era is one of the best tourist attractions in the West. It has the stamp of the farm upon it, which is most apt, for the land is Saskatchewan.

No human soul can walk on that prairie earth and be unmindful of its greatness. It pulled men to it, fed them and moulded a new breed of western man. That prairie earth which can be heavy or light has ruined men and made men. That same earth gives strength to the nation. Without it there would be no nation from sea to sea, without it Canada would not rank so high among the trading nations of the world. When the men who till that earth are unhappy over yield or price the political tempo of the nation's capital quickens. When all is well and the cargoes on their way, the logistics

Saskatchewan has always been close to the Mounties . . .

of transportation are changed. The stevedore and the sailor on the Atlantic and Pacific coasts are vitally interested in what happens in the prairie earth. Wars, skirmishes, political upheavals and fallen heroes are all part of her influence. This friendly earth which will challenge a pickaxe but allow a tiny kernel of wheat to dig deep has brought despair and delight to thousands.

Those who think the prairie is endless, flat and dull should come to Saskatchewan and stand alone on the spreading earth under the unsoiled skies. There are stretches of flatness, yes, but have you seen the prairie on a windy day? Now she is restless and the golden tipped waves rise and fall across the land. All that is needed are white breakers to make it a twin of the oceans. The shadows of the clouds flirt and skip across the flowing land, the wind whispers and spirals the dust, and far ahead are the changing colours of brown fallow soil and the rigid patterns of plough and planter.

When the wheatfields are bent by the westerly winds, only the sloping sentinels, the grain elevators, stand unmoved—silhouetted against the shifting sky. They point like swords to the boundless canopy of the skies. Sentinels they are called, but barometers they are. When they cluster beside the railroad tracks, that is an indicator of the yield of the earth. When they stand with sloping shoulders alone, the land is poor. The prosperity of towns is often told by the number of elevators. These tall, silent barometers now have a rival on the sky line—the oil-drilling rigs, since Saskatchewan is now the second biggest producer of oil and gas in Canada.

Saskatchewan is only partly covered with prairie, indeed most of the province is park land or forest. The park lands are in between the grassland of the open prairie and the northern forests with their maze of lakes and rivers and Pre-Cambrian rock. These park lands make an easy transition from south to north. Actually, Saskatchewan has more lakes per capita than any other province and claims the fourth longest river which cuts across her entire width. On the United States border the highest point in the Cypress Hills is higher than the elevation at the railroad station in Banff. The most striking view in all of Saskatchewan is from this 4,546 foot top of the Cypress Hills. This freakish mound in the ranching country of southern Saskatchewan is a living museum of natural history with semi-tropical trees and plant life of species which flourished millions of years ago.

The prairie earth pulled men to it, fed them, and moulded a new breed of western man

Wheat is still king in the heart of Canada's west, but some very impressive contenders have been casting shadows over the throne. Oil and gas are now big business, and sodium sulphate, salt and potash are produced in growing quantities. But far beyond the prairie in the Pre-Cambrian shield comes the greatest of all energy producers—uranium. At the end of 1956, before the major Ontario fields came into production, Saskatchewan produced more than 60 per cent of Canada's uranium. The mining camps of the north are spurring plans for roads and services and there is hopeful talk about pulp and paper mills and hydro developments down north. Prince Albert, the jumping-off city of the north, is buzzing with activity as new empires are being thrust upon the wilderness.

Grey Owl, the canny naturalist, chose Prince Albert National Park area to live and study for his books on the outdoors. Near the camp site where he lived is Lake Waskesiu, the centre of recreational life in Prince Albert National Park. This is undoubtedly the friendliest and most democratic park in the national chain. The reason, it's in Saskatchewan. Farmers roll up in the dust-stained cars which are so common on the prairies, portable sleeping shacks are erected by the park and rented and everyone seems to have a glorious time en masse. Another favourite retreat in south central Saskatchewan is Lake Manitou, a mineral-fed lake as salty as Salt Lake itself. It is Canada's safest swimming pool because it is so buoyant the swimmers float on top. If a swimmer jumps into the water, he will pop up like a cork. The native youth like to have their pictures taken while floating on the water, reading a newspaper, and smoking a cigar.

Regina has a lake, too, only it is man made. Citizens of the Queen City are very proud of this lake which forms a mirror for the imposing legislative buildings and the gardens around it, for which all the shrubs and trees had to be imported. Visitors should not miss a trip through this house of government. The Museum of Natural History in Regina reveals the great varieties of landscapes in Saskatchewan as well as the animal and plant life. This display deflates the impression so many outsiders have of Saskatchewan as only a vast prairie.

Saskatchewan has always been close to the Royal Canadian Mounted Police and Regina remains an important administrative and training centre. The Mounties run a museum which travellers contend is one of the most

Wheat is still king . . .
but some very impressive
contenders have been
casting shadows
over the throne

educational and intriguing in Canada. In this museum has been gathered the early romantic history of the force. The Mounties in Regina are very public relations minded and welcome visitors who can inspect the rope that hanged Louis Riel, the gun of the Mad Trapper, and a great assortment of Indian and Eskimo tools and weapons. The uniforms of the early Mounties, kyaks, knives, crude instruments and some of the latest crime detection techniques are in the R.C.M.P. museum. Nearby is a Mountie chapel in honour of Maritime Province men who served in the force. The R.C.M.P. breed and train their horses at Fort Walsh in the Cypress Hills of south Saskatchewan.

Saskatoon is the belle of the plains. She sits with splendour on the south Saskatchewan. The Bessborough Hotel, which dominates her profile, has a most delightful plume of white smoke coming from her black turret which, at a distance, resembles a lazy volcano. The river is crossed by many bridges which have been tastefully designed. Coming off the lone prairie into Saskatoon is like visiting an oasis or a city on the Danube. The name Saskatoon comes from the blueberries which thrive in this area and Saskatoon pie is said to be so succulent that emigrés will choke with nostalgia at the very mention of the word.

Visitors will find Saskatchewan refreshing and full of surprises. It does not fit the school textbook picture of flat plains and six-horse teams. The only really flat part is on the Regina Plains and, as for horses, you can drive all day through the wheat lands and rarely see one. The tractor is king now. Life on the prairies can be strenuous and a big gamble but there are compensations. The bird and animal life is abundant, so most adult males know the thrill of stalking across the crunchy floor in search of partridge, geese and ducks. The sloughs and stubble attract birds by the millions on the flyway south. Nearly every prairie boy knows the fun of snaring gophers or shooting them with a twenty-two rifle. An energetic people are the natives of Saskatchewan, who have time between the seasons for a most intense social life, who think little of travelling fifty or sixty miles to attend a dance. Around the wheat pool local, the farmers' union or school house, the discussion clubs meet. No people in other parts of Canada spend so much time discussing the United Nations or world affairs as they do in Saskatchewan. Life on the prairies demands self-reliance; life in Saskatchewan is vigorous.

126

ALBERTA

9: ALBERTA

THE LARGEST FAMILY of gamblers in Canada call Alberta home. The whole province has been gambling ever since it received a provincial charter in 1905. From the look of the boom, the burgeoning cities, highways, homes and skyscrapers, the gamble has paid off. It wasn't always that way, but it would be useless to warn an Albertan about past experience because he is the greatest optimist in Canada.

Of course if "things go right" he has a lot to be optimistic about. He figures that in the long run he can't lose. What matter if the hailstones cut down his wheat or the price for beef on the hoof drops or he drills a dry hole? There are other holes; next year's crop is going to be better, and the price of beef is bound to improve. Besides, if things get too tough he can always go up to Banff and relax. If a chinook comes and breathes warm air down his neck, well, spring must not be far away. Charming boosters are the Albertans, whether they inhabit the Peace River, the short grass country, the eerie dinosaur lands or the big towns.

What is the reason for this chamber of commerce tub-thumping? Is it the altitude? Alberta is a little closer to heaven than any provinces to the east. Natives of course will interpret this in the Alberta fashion—and I must confess that when the mountain spires are flooded with the flame of morning sun and the clouds put a halo around them, it is a heavenly sight. Maybe their attitude is an amalgam of many things which make the Albertans so ebullient and so sure.

Despite the hazards of hail, frost, dry holes and falling commodity prices, Alberta is one of the dazzling rich states of the world. The total population is equivalent to the city of Toronto, but what wealth it has to share! Name it and Alberta has it. About all the province lacks is a salt water port. Even the Rockies, which provide vacation retreats without equal on the continent, work twice for Alberta—once as a playground and then as a huge natural reservoir. Without melting snows of the Rockies slowly feeding into

the Saskatchewan River system, the development of agriculture and cheap power would be insignificant.

A professor of geography from the University of Toronto once predicted that in the next 50 years Alberta would hold half the population of Canada. He spoke of the energy sources and the arable land which runs far into the country of the midnight sun. The only major energy Alberta lacks is uranium. However, the imposing uranium fields of Saskatchewan are not far away and most of them are supplied from Edmonton. Alberta has oil, gas, coal, water power, salt, forests and the tar sands of Athabaska which will feed the energy-hungry world when scientists discover an economic process of separating the sand from the oil. The future wealth of these sands is staggering.

At the moment chemical engineers are hoping to fire an atomic blast in the tar sands far below the earth's surface. The heat from this nuclear furnace will liberate the oil from the sands and give Alberta a lake of low-cost oil which could startle the markets of the world. Everything about Alberta is in grand dimensions. The mountains, weather, land and resources are big. The perennial problem of this half-mountain, half-prairie province is to find a balance between her resources, and with diversification of farming and the development of secondary industry the solution to her problem is near.

For all its potential wealth and post-war developments, Alberta still remains quite far behind the Ontario standard of living. It is still predominantly an agricultural province. Despite all the razzle-dazzle of the Calgary Stampede and the big talk of oil men, Alberta is a conservative province. It is less United Nations conscious than Saskatchewan and never quite in tune with the Ottawa line. It is the most provincial of the three prairie provinces because of the occupation and religious background of the people. Ranchers are always independent except when they want concessions from governments. They are a breed of their own and they have left a heavy brand on the hide of Alberta.

Alberta is the most Bible conscious of all the provinces. The present premier, his predecessor, and indeed the Social Credit Party grew out of Bible classes. Alberta undoubtedly has more sects or religious groups than any other of Canada's provinces. Politically, one of the strongest religious

groups in Alberta is the Mormons whose spiritual centre is to the south in Salt Lake City, Utah. The devout Mormons, with a temple in southern Alberta, deny themselves the use of coffee, tea, carbonated beverages, liquor and cigarettes. Church activities draw them into a tight family and any politician, especially in southern Alberta, must be very conscious of these deeply religious people.

The Mormons came to Alberta in the land hungry days from Utah and states to the south. Alberta can thank the thrifty Mormons for its irrigation schemes and the modern method of strip farming which reduces wind erosion across the rolling plains. Alberta is perhaps the most America orientated of all the provinces, not only because of the Mormons but because of the inordinately large number of United States citizens living there. In the great rush for land around the turn of the century, many American farm families moved into Alberta and, after World War II, thousands more came for the oil boom. The oil fields attracted the itinerant oil worker and his family and the oil tycoon—Cadillac and all. Calgary has thousands of American oil experts who will stay as long as the wells are paying. The social clubs in Calgary are loaded with these affluent Americans most of whom retain their U.S. citizenship and show little interest in national affairs. While they may be criticized on this count, it must be remembered that it was their knowledge and willingness to gamble which developed the oil wealth of Alberta. Along with the strict principles of the Mormons, the devoutness of the Bible groups, the Hutterites and other sects, the American colony in Alberta has contributed to making this province a little different from the others.

The new American colony in Alberta, despite its nostalgic bleat for Texas and Oklahoma, seems happy living in the shadow of the Rockies. The glorious retreat of Banff is only two hours drive from Calgary, and what poor soul would not be inspired with Banff and her mountain bowl and the delights of the high country? In winter Banff sparkles at every turn of the eye, and some day will be one of the world's great winter playgrounds. Some day quick transportation will pull people out of the crowded cities of North America and loose them in this vast bowl of sun, snow, mountains and clean crisp air. Few accessible places in the world have such spectacular sights and slopes and bracing climate. Skiers can zoom down the mountain

. . . *the original peoples*

slopes and then refresh themselves in hot sulphur pools which boil out of the rocks.

Banff in summer is known to every travel agent. Two decades ago it was a carriage trade town where the idle rich arrived in style and then relaxed in the trails and mountain passes. In this democratic age most visitors, schoolteacher, secretary, factory manager and family man, come on rubber wheels and through package tours. The plexi-glass sightseeing buses equipped with guide and loudspeaker rumble along the mountain roads, stopping to point out mountain goats or to feed the bears who come to the roadside. Banff in summer is highly commercialized. Life in the C.P.R.'s Banff Springs Hotel can be very swish, with the carriage trade still wearing black tie and listening to a string quartette after dinner. Down town it can be sport shirt or Bermuda shorts, and in the camping grounds of Banff National Park anything goes. The automobile has changed Banff and each year more and more people come to play in this kingdom of scenic delight.

Banff can be both commercial and absorbing as is any resort town on the continent, but the wise traveller will make his own discoveries. Banff is loaded with characters and curiosities. How many tourists walk across the Bow River bridge without seeing a sign which proclaims that this is a genuine "Indian Trading Post"? The proprietor of the Indian Trading Post is Norman Luxton, one of the grand old mountaineers and characters of the century. Norman is most disarming because he looks like a poor old character seeking a helping hand, but Norman Luxton knows more about Indians, furs, mountain legends, and characters past and present than anyone in Banff. He is a veritable walking encyclopedia.

Norman is also a sailor. In his youth he left the mountains and sailed across the Pacific Ocean in a dug-out canoe which he bought from the Haida Indians. The canoe reached Australia and then went around South America to Argentina, crossed the Atlantic to South Africa and eventually reached London, England. In case anyone doubts the story, the canoe is preserved in Thunderbird Park, Victoria, British Columbia. Next time you go to Traders Post to buy an Indian trinket, a fur hat, moccasin or bearskin, look up into those warm grey eyes and behold the proprietor Norman Luxton—sailor, Indian Trader, mountaineer and custodian of life in the high country.

Jasper, 150 miles across the mountains from Banff, is also colourful.

Alberta holds the key to the route through the Rockies

135

Alberta has oil . . .

136

Banff is a C.P.R. town. Jasper is a C.N.R. town and there is a world of difference. Banff, more compact and commercialized, is a captive of the mountains, but Jasper is a pin point in one enormous mountain bowl. It is colder in Jasper for it is farther north. Jasper stands alone in the strident Rockies. Its nearest big city is Edmonton, 225 miles away, but Banff is only 90 miles from Calgary. Jasper in the yawning Athabaska valley seems more primitive and remote.

The gem of the C.N.R.'s national hotel system is Jasper Park Lodge, three miles outside the town on the rim of a turquoise mountain lake. Jasper Park Lodge is as posh as resorts come but it has no staircases or elevators. The main lodge is a sprawling ranch house with dining room, lounge and offices, but the guests live in bungalows placed conveniently around the edge of the lake. Guests can dine elegantly in the main dining room or order meals or room service to the cottages with waiters delivering their wares by bicycle. Many a guest has been startled by a waiter riding his bicycle with one hand while holding a tray of soft drinks high above his head with the other hand. Bicycles are also equipped with racks which hold heated aluminium cabinets for the food. Full course dinners come by bicycle very promptly at Jasper Park Lodge.

The animals of the Rockies are part of the fascination of Alberta. In the big national parks, the deer and bears are very friendly and soon learn to accept gifts of food from tourists despite the warning signs about feeding animals. Permanent residents of Jasper and Banff have invented secured garbage cans, otherwise the wandering deer, elk and bear would carry away everything except the tin cans and bottles. Even on the golf courses, the bears are a problem. Many a golfer has wondered what happened to his ball until he discovered old bruin chewing merrily away. The bears also like to chew the rubber hose which feeds the sprinklers on the golf course. Resort managers also have trouble with pack rats who sneak into the cottages and steal anything bright and interesting, such as ear-rings, cuff-links, cigarettes and even false teeth.

The Rockies abound in flora, fauna, animal life and characters. Even in the very high country of the summer snow line, the alpine flowers bloom on every meadow. The curious eye can watch the mountain goat leap from crag to crag and sometimes see the craftiest of all creatures, the Grizzly

. . . the loneliness of the range

The Calgary Stampede is a reflection of the ranching spirit

himself. The best way to see the animal life of the Canadian Rockies is to hire a guide and go by foot or on horseback into the real hinterland of stone and pass. The mountain guides, rangers and wardens will fill you with tales of animals, storms, slides, danger and heroics. This is their life. The mountains are home to them. They are residents of Alberta and citizens of Canada but their world stops where the mountains become foothills on the edge of the prairie. Alberta knows the ranch and the mountain range.

The cities of Calgary and Edmonton are as different from each other as the Rockies are from the flat wheat lands, or the mountaineer is from the farmer. Calgary is effusive; Edmonton, the capital, is more restrained. Writers have been arguing for a long time why two cities less than 200 miles apart in such a young province should be so different. The answer is probably in climate and altitude. Calgary is higher, farther south and close to the mountains. Calgary is in the grass lands; Edmonton is on the prairie. In general terms, the ranchers developed Calgary; the fur traders, missionaries and civil servants built Edmonton.

Calgary was a cow-town and the early ranchers have seared the exotic brand of ranching on the city's escutcheon. In the early days they rolled into town—cowboy, boss man and rancher—looking for fun and games. The loneliness of the range, the vicissitudes of the game and the signals of the seasons drove them to cow-town. The cowboy is the sailor of the dry sea. The ocean sailor had a choice, but the cowpuncher of Alberta knew only one big port. The Calgary Stampede, billed as the World's Biggest Rodeo, is a reflection of that ranching spirit. Even the oil barons of 1960 who have never straddled a horse are heirs to that philosophy of whoop-la and gamble.

Another factor in the Calgary personality is the chinook. The chinook is a warm wind which blows out of the mountain passes. All big mountain countries know these warm mountain breezes where intense pressures heat the air and force it through the passes. Calgary is in the path. A chinook can hit Calgary when the temperature is 30° F. below zero and within an hour or two the snow will melt and temperatures soar. Spring comes many times during winter and the hopes of people rise, too. Edmonton is not so exposed to these dramatic and unpredictable warm winds from the mountains.

Edmonton is a capital city—more northern, more cosmopolitan in

... even the oil barons of 1960
who have never straddled a horse
are heirs to that philosophy
of whoop-la and gamble

racial background. Up until World War II, Edmonton was more concerned with civil servants, wheat farmers, immigrants and intrepid men going into the cold north beyond, none of whom were as gay as the cowpokes around Calgary. The peasants from northern Europe gravitated to the prairie around Edmonton, whereas the colourful remittance man from Great Britain and the cowboy from the southern states came into the foothills around Calgary. Therein lies part of the difference.

Lethbridge, the third city of Alberta, sits smugly to the south and smiles at the rivalry and antics of the two bigger cities of Alberta. Lethbridge is many times smaller than either Calgary or Edmonton, yet it has one thing in common : Lethbridge is also one of the three gateways through the Rocky Mountains. Edmonton controls the Yellowhead Pass, Calgary the Kicking Horse Pass, and Lethbridge the Crows Nest Pass. Lethbridge claims it is in the "banana belt" with less snow and trouble in crossing the mountains. The rivalry for passage over the mountains is very keen in Alberta as Ottawa knows so well. The Trans Canada Highway route was finally chosen to go through the Calgary—Kicking Horse Pass route much to the disgust of Edmonton and Lethbridge.

Edmonton may boast about her swift growth and oil fields, Calgary may claim prowess as home to oil companies and ranchers, but Lethbridge is the symbol of the boom on the Alberta farm front. Ever since its founding, Lethbridge has been known as a coal-mining town—a small town in southern Alberta surrounded by semi-productive wheatfields and dry, dry range and supported by coal miners. All this has changed, thanks to the big-gest surgical job west of the St. Lawrence Seaway. In Lethbridge one speaks of "the big ditch". Irrigation has changed the sky line and the ring of the cash register in Lethbridge; irrigation has drastically reduced the number of acres required to finish one steer; irrigation has produced mountains of sugar beets, corn, peas and market vegetables and made Lethbridge one of the principal canning areas in the whole of Canada. The sugar beet refineries now outclass the grain elevators as symbols of prosperity in southern Alberta. Lethbridge without the boom of oil or gas is growing faster propor-tionately than either Calgary or Edmonton. The boosters of Lethbridge claim the city cannot lose because, unlike oil and gas, garden crops are renewable as long as the water tumbles out of the Rockies. And Lethbridge

...the eerie dinosaur lands

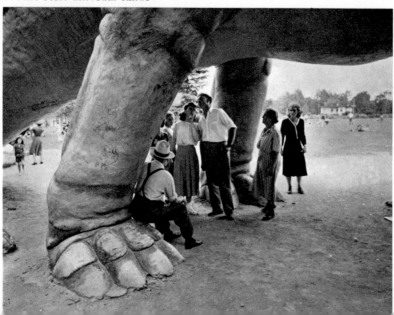

says that it, too, has a mountain haven on her western gate—Waterton Lakes, not as well publicized as Banff or Jasper but even more spectacular.

The ranch country between Lethbridge and Calgary is a travel page sequence. The Duke of Windsor, when Prince of Wales, bought a ranch in the foothills of Alberta and despite all the vicissitudes of a dethroned monarch still holds the title of Alberta rancher. Old time ranchers claim that when the Duke first saw this flaming country where the hills get down on their knees before the mountain grandeur, he said it was the most spectacular area he had ever seen. There are no quotes available but the Duke of Windsor still owns the EP ranch. This is Canada's big cattle country and the ranches sweep from the wheatlands up over the tumbling hills to the very base of the snow dusted Rockies.

High River is the capital of cowboys. Many of the pioneer ranchers and cowpokes have settled here or nearby. They would feel "awful lonesome" in any other place. For them this is the land of the big sky and big surprise. Anything can come out of those mountains—the most "cussed weather" and the most glorious of sights. Here above the 49th parallel they can winter graze the cattle, shoot mountain lions and grizzlies, catch trout in the streams which cut the ranches, and still grow wheat and gamble on oil and gas wells. The twin enemies are weather and government. The Alberta rancher must run from the weather but he will run to the government only when he has to.

Not so many years ago Alberta government bonds were shunned by broker and buyer throughout North America. Today, Alberta is the most debt-free state on the continent. Today, gas from below the wheatfields of Alberta fires the furnaces of Montreal and Toronto. Today, oil from below the tumbling foothills drives the automobiles of Canadians from Victoria to Montreal. The old and colourful gamble on wheat and cattle has been minimized with the development of the oil, gas and allied manufacturing industries. Southern Alberta has mixed and specialized farming, thanks to irrigation, and northern Alberta is poised for the dawn of stupendous developments down north. Alberta holds the key to the routes through the Rockies, but the greatest rôle of all may be the road to northern riches. Canada spreads for two full time zones west and north of Alberta. Alaska and the Yukon and the whole northwest are linked with Edmonton. Edmonton is the base city of highway or flyway. Go west, young man, go west.

THE WALL OF ROCK between the prairies and the Pacific Ocean has been cursed by explorer, railroader and sky pilot. The wall could more accurately be called a sea of mountains but is casually and inaccurately referred to as "the Rockies".

On the western side of this wall is the fastest growing of all the provinces of Canada, British Columbia, big, brash and burly, whose phenomenal growth even confounds the natives.

The oldest citizens of Vancouver can remember the city as a saw-mill village on Burrard Inlet. The real old timers can remember when the first train came down the western slope of the mountains to link British Columbia to the rest of Canada. The growth of this city west of the forbidding wall of rock is like a dream—incredible that in one span of human existence this shack town should become the third largest city in Canada. Maisonneuve had laid the foundations of a permanent settlement in Montreal 244 years before Vancouver was incorporated.

The spectacular rise of this dazzling city on the Pacific side of the mountains has made her more conscious than ever of the wall of rock which separates her from the east. Vancouver grew lusty without being rich. Before World War II Vancouver was the largest city of a province which just missed falling into the "have-not" class. The older and more secure cities of the east, with their solid head offices, rankled this bubbling child on the other side of "the Rockies". Dependence on the east turned the sea of rocks into a psychological wall.

The wall is still there and Vancouver, the most self-conscious of all Canadian cities, wails and rails against it. Visitors from eastern Canada, in all innocence, usually gasp at the setting and relish the tales of dynamic expansion, but within a few hours they are made to feel like strangers in a different land. Vancouver carries a chip on the shoulder. Vancouverites make all eastern Canadians feel apologetic for living in the "less favoured" lands east of

. . . this is the real life

the mountains. Far away Ottawa seems to be the devil incarnate with no appreciation of the problems beyond the mountains. Toronto's grasping hands hold the mortgage, and the prairie folk should know better than to live in their Siberian misery. Vancouver is smug—or is it really trying to rationalize the role of being far out on the western limb of Canada?

Vancouver in terms of tempo, climate and space is almost as far from Ottawa as Ottawa is from London, England. Vancouver has all the problems of the growing adolescent in relation to his parents, but who can blame this precocious child for being a little assertive? See her when the mountains are proud of defending her—see this city when the ocean sparkles delight at guarding her—see Vancouver when the soft breezes waft her, and then you will believe that this is the queen of all cities. The adjectives will roll off the tongue—majestic, peerless, beautiful and unique—that is Vancouver. Young, refreshing, vigorous can be added to the list. Indeed, Vancouver's main difficulty, despite occasional dampening factors from the ocean beyond her, is that she is too far away from other Canadian cities of comparable size.

The native and the transplanted citizens of Canada's third largest city will declare under oath that this is the real life—boating all the year, skiing in snow-capped mountains and golfing the same day within the confines of the city. Sure, the mountains force the clouds to drop their moisture frequently, but isn't that better than sloshing through snow and huddling for warmth? When people in the other parts of Canada are tending furnaces, the West Coast Canadian is tending his boats and roses in the gardens. Climate, scenery and opportunity are all here, so can we blame these Pacific Coast Canadians for being a little smug? Throw away your galoshes, red flannel drawers and eastern ways—"Come west, Canadians, come west" is the cry of those who have seen the light in the far western sky.

Many Canadians think of British Columbia as if it were composed solely of Vancouver and Victoria. This is fuzzy thinking because neither city, especially Vancouver, could survive without the rich hinterland within and beyond the mountain ranges. Cities cannot live unto themselves. British Columbia, however, has the most lopsided of all populations because more than 75 per cent of all British Columbians live in less than five per cent of the total area of the province. Three quarters of all the people in British Columbia live in the metropolitan areas of Vancouver and Victoria. The wealth which supports this urban octopus comes from the sea, the mountain valleys, plateaus, benchlands and hinterland in general.

Inland from the coast are some of the world's largest mineral deposits, water power resources, timber stands, grazing lands and orchards. The "interior", as they call it in British Columbia, holds the hope chest for the whole province. Development of hydro-electric power in British Columbia amazes most eastern Canadians but at the present booming rate it may take 100 years to utilize the potential. British Columbia is the third largest province in Canada, but in terms of topographical and climatic range it has no peer. On a straight line from Prince Rupert to Ashcroft, the full range of climate is seen; Prince Rupert is soaked with rain but Ashcroft is so dry that sage brush and cactus grow. Kitimat on the coast produces aluminium ingots because the electricity made from water is cheap, but in arid-irrigated Osoyoos rattle snakes slip between melons measuring four feet long.

British Columbia pulls her wealth from the ocean, the mountains, the valleys and the great grasslands of the interior. B.C., despite her salt water sailors and lumberjacks, is home to the cowboy. Provincial patriots proclaim that the ranches of this province are bigger than anything in Alberta or Texas. The Douglas Lake Ranch, 140 miles north-east of Vancouver claims 650,000 acres of wild grasses, benchlands, valleys and fields of alfalfa and timothy. The fences protecting this range would stretch in a straight line from Montreal to Halifax. There are whole empires of grass beyond the mountains in British Columbia. The Calgary Stampede would be shorthanded without participating cowboys from British Columbia. Even a Texan or an Argentinian would get lost in the B.C. cow country beyond the mountains.

British Columbia has two climates—oceanic and continental. The moist, warm air from the Pacific makes her western slopes a kingdom of trees— trees so big and tall that her lumberjacks regard the eastern Canadian woodsmen as sissies playing with matches. The same mountain wall which isolates this province from the rest of Canada and makes B.C. insular in thought is also the judge between ocean and continent weather. The mountains search the fleeing clouds and drain them of moisture. South-eastern British Columbia—beyond the coastal range—is dry like Sahara, and plants will grow only when irrigation is applied. The winters are temperate and the summers dry and hot.

. . . a kingdom of trees

The Okanagan Valley, which produces so many of Canada's apples, can be so hot that the sand on the beaches will burn the soles of the feet. The hills are brown with sage brush in summer. In the Okanagan, every fruit grower is at the mercy of the water flumes which bring life down from the mountains. Northwest of the Okanagan, ranchers pray for rain. The common denominator of British Columbia is the lack of or the abundance of water. No people in Canada are so water conscious. Salt water brings the salmon to her shores, rain water makes the trees fat and tall, melting snow spins the turbines which in turn make metal out of minerals and newsprint out of logs. Where there is no water, there is worry. B.C. has both. Water brings British Columbia into international forums. Harnessed water makes Vancouver the most gaily-lit city in Canada. Potential water power in the far north attracts the richest entrepreneurs on earth. In the dry belts—away from the coast—water is all but measured by the spoonful.

Moisture is the key to this continental-oceanic province. Moisture is the servant of the mountains. Far to the north, where the land is prairie, the winters are less severe than they are in Winnipeg, hundreds of miles south. Away up east of the mountains, wheat will ripen two weeks ahead of the southern prairie because of the long days of sunshine. The Rockies are lower in the northern reaches of B.C., and so the warm moist currents from the Pacific flow east. Northern prairie British Columbia—the Peace River country—experiences Chinook winds just as Calgary does. These springlike breezes flow out of the mountain passes and in a few hours will change the temperature from 10° F. below to 40° F. above. Edmonton, Alberta, can be frigid when the weather man talks of much higher temperatures along the Alaska Highway in British Columbia.

This vast prairie and foothill hinterland has now been linked to the coast by railroad. It may yet prove to be the powerhouse of the province because the developments in oil and gas have been spectacular and pipe lines now bend across the mountains. It looks as if the British Columbia story has come full circle because the Peace River country was the gateway for the first settlements in the province. The explorers—MacKenzie, Fraser and Thompson—and the fur traders themselves came to British Columbia overland over the obvious route, Peace River. Today, the province looks once again to the north-eastern corner—toward the route of the overlanders.

Edmonton may boast that the Alaska Highway is almost at her gates but this is chamber of commerce talk because the Alaska Highway does not touch the province of Alberta. It winds northwest for more than 600 miles through British Columbia before it enters the Yukon. The extension of the Pacific Great Eastern Railroad to Dawson Creek, B.C. means that the rich cattle, grain and oil country of northern Alberta now has an outlet to the Pacific through British Columbia. West of the Peace River country, towards the Pacific, British Columbia contemplates the most gigantic hydro projects of all. A relief map of Canada's third largest province shows only a few scratches in the name of civilization. Veritable empires of forest, stream and ore-laden mountains wait for the engineer and entrepreneur. The coastal cities may sing about the broad Pacific and trade with the teeming oriental world across it, but there would be little to ship if British Columbia could not look inland.

"The interior" is a nice coastal expression which covers the whole of the province except the Pacific shoreline. The interior includes the lead, zinc, copper, silver, gold which pours out of the Kootenay's; the apples, peaches and pears of the Okanagan; the small fruits and dairy products from the Fraser Valley; cattle and hides from the grasslands; lumber from every handy slope and even coal from the Crow's Nest Pass. If it were not for the Fraser River, which is born in "the interior", there would be no salmon fishermen at its mouth. The salmon too wants to get into "the interior" in order to propagate the species. The salmon's do and die effort is copied by the coast ports of Vancouver, New Westminster, Victoria, Powell River, Kitimat, Prince Rupert and the rest.

With immense wealth tumbling down from the interior upon a small urban population, British Columbia must export or burst. Production in British Columbia is on a massive scale. If every resident of the province ate nothing but salmon three times each day, there would still be enough left over to supply a dozen republics of Latin America. Productivity in B.C. has global proportions. The fertilizer produced at Trail could smother the arable land of the province and that is why it is used to grow pineapples in Hawaii, tea in Malaya, garden crops in India and wheat on the Regina Plains. Okanagan apples are favourites in Piccadilly Circus; Powell River newsprint becomes a scandal sheet in Mexico City; Prince George plywood makes walls

Splinters from the Orient have drifted ashore at Vancouver

for homes in equatorial Africa. The primary and secondary resource products must move out of the province. Vancouver is the third largest city in Canada because it is the manager, broker, shipper and frequently financier of a rich array of natural resources—most of them within the mountains but some along the coast too. Coast and interior are interlocked. The interior would wither without portals to the world and so would those portals shrink without the produce from within.

The ledger of productivity and transportation is kept in the capital city of Victoria. Most Canadians from Vancouver east to St. John's, Newfoundland, smile with reservation when the word Victoria is mentioned. Most Canadians see Victoria as a stuffy outpost of imperial splendour. Canadians smile because they feel this is the last stand of the Colonel Blimps and pukka-pukka colonials. It is true that the Empress Hotel serves tea and crumpets every afternoon while the orchestra captures the mood of Queen Victoria's day. True it is that the gentlemen wear blue blazers with regimental insignia firmly sewn on the left front pocket; true that many of the ladies arrive in long gowns and the whole coterie of tea lovers discuss the state of the Commonwealth. Victoria does attract the retired British officer and it is true he is more British than the British of Great Britain. No one has ever had the courage to say why these Britishers who served overseas and who kept a nostalgic line with home never went back to Great Britain upon retirement.

They could have returned home to Britain, or they could have stayed in Hong Kong, New Delhi and Rangoon but they selected Victoria, Canada. There was no financial advantage because the pensions were in pounds sterling and not dollars; indeed the difference between the devalued pound and the princely Canadian dollar must hurt these relaxed Britishers who settle in Victoria. Their presence in this capital city of British Columbia is a living tribute to the climate and ways of Victoria, and mainland Canadian visitors suspect that the Victorians are rather glad these ardent Britishers picked this spot.

The remittance man and the service man have brought to Victoria a love of life and high degree of intelligence. They represent only a small percentage of the city's population but they have left a fine mark upon the escutcheon of Victoria. Victoria is the most aesthetically-minded city we have in Canada and certainly the most cause-conscious. Look in the "letters to the

The word "culture" is popular in British Columbia

editor" columns of the two newspapers and you will understand. Most national telecasters and radio personalities know that people in Victoria do more than spend time sipping tea and rolling black balls across green grass. Make one slip about a rhododendron or Rhode Island pullet and Victoria will fume. No city in Canada can match Victoria for tourist promotion. Many visitors claim that Victoria is far more Canadian than Vancouver since she does not try to copy Seattle and San Francisco but just acts herself. The British touches are here; neat gardens, clipped hedges, banks of flowers and hounds on leashes. However, the main streets and buildings of Victoria have the big open vistas of any western city. Victoria does not look English at all but is a Canadian city with very fine touches added.

Life in Victoria is not hard to take. Nature has been most benign to this medium-sized city and the residents have made intelligent use of it. The tender care taken in private gardens, lawns, hedges and the fine public parks and playgrounds is proof that Victoria wants to enjoy nature and improve it. Even the prairie farmer who comes to Victoria to fill out his span of life soon catches the spirit of relaxation, whether it be in gardening, yachting, fishing or golfing. Victoria is rich in recreational facilities. The climate helps develop this mood, but so does the livelihood of the city. Victoria is a provincial capital and civil servants are never in a rush, no matter how dedicated and hard working some of them are. Victoria is a naval town, and the navy on shore is never too worried about clocks.

One of Victoria's major exports is selling her climate, scenery and recreational facilities to Canadians who live in less favourable climates. This is Canada's California, and each month the population grows from Canadian couples who wish to slacken the pace and make those last few years roll gently. Even from as far east as Quebec the older citizens relish the retired life of Victoria. Picking your own daffodils when the rest of Canada is shivering has its own rewards. A golf ball really sails above the fairway in February. These retired but permanent residents of Victoria and Vancouver Island add to the leisurely charm of the evergreen playground.

Eastern Canadians may suspect that Victoria is dull or dead from all these retired people. Far from it. Victoria is pleasant, restful and at times zestful without being tiring. The capital city has a happy blend of business and pleasure. It makes money from tourists and has one of the most progressive

Victoria . . . a happy blend of business and pleasure

tourist operations in Canada, the Victoria and Island Publicity Bureau, managed by that master promoter, George Warren. But manufacturing is still the biggest revenue producer. Victoria has shipyards, saw mills, paint factories and many small firms. Victoria is also a big lumber town because the great forests stretch above her and she has been so skilful in blending them with the joy of living. All the Canadians who come to live on Vancouver Island are not infirm or even old. The active capitalist and writer come here, too. After all, Victoria is a growing community full of opportunity and the easy climate and recreational facilities are extra inducements. Bruce Hutchinson and Stuart Keate are nationally known writers and though they could command top positions on any newspaper in Canada, even a breeches-buoy could not pull them off the island of Vancouver.

Geography pulls some neat tricks on the layman in British Columbia. Canadians talk about the east-west line from St. John's, Newfoundland, to Victoria, as if Victoria were due west from Vancouver. It is not straight west. It is almost due south of Vancouver. Victoria has the most moderate climate in Canada but in terms of Windsor, St. Catharines and even Montreal it is several hundred miles to the north. The Okanagan Valley, north of the conventional 49th parallel, is a surprise because it is boiling hot and dry in summer and as lush as California when water is brought to the land. When the coastal British Columbian is saturated with fog and liquid sunshine, the Saharas of the interior will soon evaporate the moisture. These dry valleys are just a few hours drive from the Pacific.

The climate from the western slope of the Rockies to the coast draws the adventurer, worker, pensioner, loafer, eccentric, remittance man, sybarite and the lost soul. British Columbia must have the highest ratio of "characters" to total population of any province in Canada. California has a similar ratio of individualism. The Canadian unemployables can survive better in Vancouver. The interior towns have their quota of unusual types who refuse to be crushed by the onslaught of North American materialism. Whether they be hermits, lonely ranchers, cricket breeders, horticulturists, poets, nature lovers or religious fanatics, British Columbia attracts them. They all add to the cultural yeast of this most westerly province. A nudist colony could not get a bare toe-hold in Ontario, but in B.C. anything goes as long as the mountains and the ocean remain—as long as the trees grow tall, the

. . . the easy climate and recreational facilities are added inducements

salmon run, the orchards survive and the Pacific sends forth her warm breath.

The word culture is popular in British Columbia. It means the arts as well as a way of life. Living is the important thing whether it be cruising the Gulf Islands, picnicking in Stanley Park, climbing Mount Seymour, pulling salmon from the Capilano, skiing on Forbidden Plateau, driving through Cathedral Grove, attending the Vancouver Festival of the Arts or as a retired banker skipping a curling rink in Nelson. The citizens of the southern coast can play in the outdoors almost every day of the year. They are not forced to take golf lessons indoors or wait for May to ready the boat or cottage. They can play all the time, or at least when the sunshine is not too moist. Can we blame them for being a little smug? After all, Ottawa is far, far away, beyond the mountains.

Living is the important thing

C O L O P H O N :

The photographs by Yousuf Karsh
have been reproduced by the gravure process
at the works of
Sun Printers Limited, Watford, Hertfordshire, England.
The words by John Fisher have been set
in a type called Pilgrim, a cutting by
Linotype and Machinery Limited of England
from the Bunyan type of Eric Gill.
The binding was done by
Hazell Watson and Viney Limited, Aylesbury and London.
The book was designed by
the Canadian typographer Carl Dair. FTDC